Jack Fi

A Rugby League

Gary Slater

London League Publications Ltd

Jack Fish
A Rugby League superstar

A CIP catalogue record for this book is available from the British Library.

First published in Great Britain in April 2012 by:
London League Publications Ltd, P.O. Box 65784, London NW2 9NS

ISBN: 978-1903659-61-8

Cover design by: Stephen McCarthy Graphic Design
                               46, Clarence Road, London N15 5BB

Layout: Peter Lush

Printed and bound in Great Britain by Charlesworth Press, Wakefield

Foreword

Jack Fish was my grandfather and although I never met him, because he died before I was born, I have always felt that I knew him. Whenever I visited my Auntie Alice, Jack's daughter, I was told what a great player he was: how popular with the supporters, how they put him on a pedestal, how fast he was on the field, how many tries he scored. Even now I am emotional when I see stories about him in the newspapers and delighted that his exploits have not been forgotten.

Jack lived at 10 York Street, Warrington, in a very ordinary and small, terraced house. Rugby league players – and especially footballers – are more upper crust these days but Jack and his team-mates were much more down to earth. On the wall over the sideboard there was a photograph of Jack in a lovely, big oval frame. He was pictured in his rugby kit inside a plaice with the words: "Play up Warrington! Are we downhearted? No, we have a Fish to plaice a try." I will always remember that andthat the picture had pride of place.

In Jack's day there were plenty of visitors. He was good friends with George Formby senior, the entertainer, and he used to pop round for a chat. George Formby junior used to take my dad, another Jack, for a walk around Latchford while the two men had a conversation. They probably met at an official club dinner and remained friends after that. Lady Frances Greenall, of the Greenall Whitley brewing family who lived at Walton Hall, was another regular visitor. When she came round the best crockery came out.

It was said that, sometimes, Jack would throw up at the side of the pitch before a match, maybe through nerves, maybe through drink. Who knows? My dad, who only died in November 2010, aged 93, did not like to talk about Jack too much because he said it sounded like he was bragging or boasting, but he would never part with his memorabilia, his Lancashire cap, his South West Lancashire winners' medal and various photographs and newspaper cuttings. He said that pub landlords in Warrington used to advertise if Jack was going in that night and the place would be packed; that's how popular he was. There was a photograph of Jack on the wall in the Britannia pub, which is where I met my husband, Ken.

In the 1950s, supporters used to argue about who was the better player, Jack Fish or Brian Bevan, but unless you saw them both play at their peak it must be impossible to decide. My family and I have always been proud of Jack and his achievements and that can never be taken away. Even now people still say that my granddad was a famous rugby player. So I am delighted that now, for the first time, a book has been written about his life and career. My dad would be very proud.

Barbara Bibby

About the author

Gary Slater was born in Warrington in 1961, five days before the Wire played Leeds in the Championship Final at Odsal. He watched his first Warrington games on television before finally going to Wilderspool for the first time, aged 10, with his uncle, Derek Hill, for a Challenge Cup replay against Castleford in 1972. Warrington won 12–5, thanks to a try from Brian Brady, and he has been supporting the club ever since.

Warrington have been to five Challenge Cup finals at Wembley since then and Gary has been to them all, firstly as a supporter and later as a journalist with the *Warrington Guardian* and *The Daily Telegraph*.

His early playing heroes were Alex Murphy and John Bevan but he became fascinated by Jack Fish while researching his second book *Warrington RLFC 100 Greats*, which he co-wrote with photographer Eddie Fuller in 2002. His first book, *Warrington RLFC 1970-2000*, also co-written with Eddie Fuller, was published in 2000, reprinted in 2004 and revised and reprinted in 2010.

A third book, *So close to Glory, Warrington RLFC 1919 to 1939*, was published by London League Publications Ltd in 2008. Now living in London, Gary has four sons, all of whom are Warrington supporters.

Acknowledgements

This book, like all books about rugby league, has been a labour of love. No author ever got rich by writing about the 13-man code. Still, the project has been a joy from start to finish and thanks are due to a whole host of people.

Peter Lush and Dave Farrar of London League Publications Ltd showed faith in the idea. Neil Dowson, of Warrington Wolves, gave encouragement and supplied photographs, as did Mike Parsons, of the *Warrington Guardian*. Stan Lewandowski, of the Warrington Past Players' Association, unearthed some fascinating cuttings, cartoons and photographs.

Thanks also to Steve McCarthy for designing the cover, Peter Lush for doing the lay-out and the staff of Charlesworth Press for printing the book.

Finally, thanks to Bob Brough and Eddie Fuller for their photographic skills and, most importantly, to Jack Fish's family for their passion and patience.

Gary Slater

Introduction

Jack Fish was one of rugby league's first star players but he was also a larger-than-life figure and a colourful, complex and sometimes controversial character. That is what makes him so interesting. He scored the first try in rugby league's first international match and was one of the first players to score 1,000 points in the new code of rugby, following the breakaway from the Rugby Football Union to form the Northern Union.

He was Warrington's first superstar and even now, 100 years after his last appearance and 70 years after his death, he remains the only man to have scored 200 tries and kicked 200 goals for the club.

He was a match-winner who had style, swagger and charisma. The supporters loved him and often wore metal fish-shaped badges to big matches to show their devotion. They also wrote poems and limericks about him and his exploits.

With Fish on the left wing, the Wirepullers of Warrington reached four Challenge Cup finals in seven seasons, winning two and losing two. When they won the Cup for the first time, at Headingley in 1905, Fish scored both their tries in a 6–0 victory over Hull Kingston Rovers.

Two years later, Fish was the captain as Warrington beat Oldham 17–3 in the final at Wheater's Field, Broughton. Fish scored an amazing try and kicked four goals.

Like all great wingers, Fish had pace to burn. But he also had three extra attributes which made him stand apart from his rivals. He possessed a baffling side-step, a remarkable swerve and, most famously of all, the ability to stop dead while running at full speed and then regain top speed again almost immediately. Sometimes this sent opponents whizzing into touch, sometimes it left them trying to tackle thin air. One player, after being beaten by the Warrington winger all afternoon, complained: "I believe Fish could dodge death itself."

On another occasion, Fish was up against Harry Taylor, Hull's outstanding full-back, who would go on to play for England and Great Britain. Fish received the ball in space at half way and so Taylor ran towards him but made no attempt to tackle the flying winger, simply running parallel with him until Fish scored near the corner flag. Tries were worth three points at the time. After the match one of the Hull directors asked Taylor why he had made no attempt at a tackle.

"I know Jack Fish only too well," Taylor replied. "Our team were only winning by four points and had I attempted to tackle him, Fish would have been certain to side-step me and score a try under the posts. As it was I made him score at the corner. The goal kick failed and Hull won the match."

Another full-back, Sam Houghton, had known Fish since they grew up together in Runcorn. Houghton was a top-class rugby player himself and played for England against Ireland in 1892 and against Wales in 1896, but still suffered against Fish. In one match at Wilderspool, in the days when the pitch was surrounded by a picket fence, Houghton was playing for Runcorn and hurled himself at Fish.

"I missed him," Houghton recalled, "but I knocked two of the railings out with my head and face. Then some enthusiast wanted to hit me with a railing!"

Fish collected many nicknames: the slippery one, the Warrington crack, the prince of scorers and the artful dodger. He was also the star attraction in Warrington's first great threequarter line – Fish, Isherwood, Dickenson and Harris – who were known as the Aristocratic Four and whose play was described as "poetry in motion".

Fish was the first Warrington player to score five tries in a match and the first Warrington player to kick nine goals in a match. He was regularly singled out for special attention by opposing players and suffered some terrible injuries, but was never sent off.

In the days when rugby league's County Championship was an important competition, he scored 16 tries in 16 appearances for Lancashire. For Warrington, he scored tries against the touring teams from Australia and New Zealand. He also played for England and only missed out on the first Northern Union tour in 1910 to Australia and New Zealand because of injury.

Against Goole in 1900, he scored five tries and kicked seven goals for a total of 29 points – a then Northern Union record. Six years later, he scored 30 points in a match against Huddersfield.

Even after his retirement from playing his love affair with rugby league continued and in July 1927 he was appointed Warrington coach and, almost inevitably, guided the team to the Challenge Cup final in his only season in charge.

Fish's club try-scoring record of 214 remained intact for 40 years, until Brian Bevan came along, but even now the great Australian is the only Warrington player with more tries to his name. Fish and Bevan: Warrington's two greatest players, and two of the sport's greatest wingers.

Even now, Fish's exploits have not been completely forgotten. In 2003 when the Warrington Wolves Past Players' Association launched their Hall of Fame, Fish was one of 12 founding members. He is also featured in the Gillette Rugby League Heritage Centre at the George Hotel in Huddersfield. The late Ernie Day, who first collated all Warrington's records and statistics, was the first to describe Fish as Warrington's first superstar and so I owe the title of the book to him. What is more, he was exactly right. Jack Fish was Warrington's first superstar and this is his story.

Gary Slater

Contents

Appendices

Jack Fish in Lancashire kit.

1. Signing for Warrington

"I did not know there was so much money in the world"

October 1898 was a memorable month for the bustling Lancashire market town of Warrington because Barnum and Bailey's "greatest show on earth" paid a visit, fresh from its stunning success at Olympia in London.

The American circus act arrived at Warrington Bank Quay Station in the early hours of Saturday, 8 October, and, by 8am, had almost completed setting up their 12 canvas pavilions, capable of seating 15,000 people and including a magnificent big top, on a ground off Wilderspool Road – about 200 yards from Warrington Football Club's rugby ground.

Between 9am and 10am the circus set off on a parade to drum up business through the town centre where 40,000 people were lining the streets. The population of the town was only 65,000. The order of procession was as follows:

Police
Mounted Officers
Grand Military Band
Stupendous Forty-Horse United Team
Open Den of Tigers and Trainer
Open Den of Lions and Trainer
Open Den of Leopards and Trainer
Open Den of Panthers and Trainer
Open Den of Hyenas and Trainer
Open Den of Bears and Trainer
Open Den of Wolves and Trainer
Novel Melechoir Chimes, drawn by six horses
Lady Performers and Side-Saddle Experts
Mounted Ladies of the Hippodrome
Gentlemen Hippodrome Riders
Two 2-horse Roman Chariots, Lady Drivers
Two 4-horse Roman Chariots
Band Chariot "Euterpe" drawn by Ten Horses
Eight Golden Chariots containing rare wild beasts
Triumphal Chariot with queer musicians and comic heads
Caravan of Camels, with Asiatic Riders
Twenty Performing Elephants
Two Elephants with Howdahs and Oriental Beauties
Blue Beard Chariot, drawn by Six Zebras
Japanese Dragon Chariot with performers

1

Cinderella's Fairy Coach
Little Red Riding Hood Chariot
Mother Goose Chariot
Blue Band Chariot "America" drawn by Ten Horses
Seven Golden Cages containing rare animals
Mammoth Organ Chariot
Grand Triumphal Float

Columbus Section
Representing the reception for Columbus at Barcelona 400 years ago:
Royal Mace Bearers
Squad of Eight Royal Trumpeters
Grand Triumphal Throne Chariot of Ferdinand and Isabella
Mounted Grandees, Nobles, Cavaliers, Knights, Ambassadors, and prominent personages in correct, elegant and costly historical costumes
The Great Discoverer Christopher Columbus
Emblematic Float, with fruits, plants and living evidences of the new country
Steam Calliope

Among the sideshows were a giant, male and female dwarves, Johanna the gorilla and a beautiful, but bearded, lady. The people of Warrington, many of whom had not been outside Lancashire, had never seen anything like it. One wide-eyed teenager who enjoyed the fun had another reason to celebrate. His name was Jack Fish and he had been asked to sign for Warrington, one of the leading clubs in the breakaway Northern Union. Another two Northern Union clubs, Oldham and Stockport, were also showing an interest.

Fish had been born as John Fish at 7 Cooper Street, Runcorn on 30 December, 1878 and was the first child of Richard Fish, aged 25, a brickmaker's labourer, and his 22-year-old wife, Mary Ann Fish, neé Clarke. The couple had both been born in Runcorn and had been married for two years and, like most working-class people at the time, were destined to have a large family. Fish was followed by two brothers, Samuel and Edward, and five sisters – Eliza Jane, Agnes, Annie, Edith and Mary Ann.

Fish attended the Brunswick Street Wesleyan School before moving on to St Edward's Catholic School in Millbrow. Runcorn was a rugby-mad town in those days and St Edward's boasted a good team. Fish, the fastest boy in the school, was chosen on the left wing – a position he would make his own for the next 20 years. He became a prolific try scorer for his school and, in his last year there, they were crowned district champions.

At school, he learned the rules of rugby, but it was while playing with his friends that he honed his skills and learned the tricks of the trade that would make him a legend. "As lads," Fish recalled in an interview in 1938, "we used to play rugby in a narrow terrace on the side of the canal at Runcorn.

"Our 'ball' was a piece of rubber tubing about six inches in diameter, which we used to obtain from the local works. The tubing was used for running acid through, and when we took dinners to the works we used to ask one of the men to cut us a piece off, or cut off a piece ourselves if no one was looking.

"Then off to the field, which was a narrow, cinder-covered passage, with stout boards on either side. If you went down on the cinders, you got badly scarred hands and knees for your trouble, while to be pushed into touch meant that you were banged well and hearty against the boards.

"It is a wonder some of us were not killed. There was very little room when you were dashing away with the 'ball' and an opponent, sometimes much bigger than yourself, was waiting to tackle you. Many a time I was afraid I might be hurt, and I developed the habit of stopping quickly and then doubling away from the lad who was waiting to tackle me.

"I did it so often that it gradually became a gift, and one which I was to use effectively in years to come. Of course, from my youngest days I was always nimble on my feet. I had good thighs and hips, with plenty of strength in them, and my legs tapered down nicely.

"I could usually dodge the other boy in our games, but there is no doubt that it was bodily fear when we played rugby as youngsters at Runcorn that helped me to develop my side-step.

"Those games also taught me much in the art of gathering a ball which came to me at arm's length. The lads passed the piece of rubber tubing at all angles and I used to throw my arm out, gather it, and bring it in to my body as I was running, just as I used to gather difficult passes in later years in first-class rugby.

"I was fortunate, too, to have a very keen sense of sight, and this stood me in good stead during my subsequent career."

In 1891, at the age of 12, Fish left school and was one of the many boys and young men of the day whose first job was helping to make the Manchester Ship Canal, which opened in 1894.

Years later he could still vividly recall an occasion when the old river broke into the Ship Canal at Thelwall, Warrington, washing away part of the embankment and much of the material the workmen were using, and flooding the bed of the canal. Fish was one of the many workmen rushed to the district to assist in repairing the damage.

When Fish was 15, his family – along with many other Runcorn people – moved to Lostock Gralam so that he and his father Richard could work in a new chemical factory. Built by Messrs Bownman & Thompson, the factory later became Brunner Mond and is now one of the world's leading manufacturers and suppliers of soda ash, sodium bicarbonate, calcium chloride and associated alkaline chemicals.

At the time, Witton Albion and Lostock Gralam had very good football teams in the Cheshire Senior and Cheshire Junior Leagues respectively and Fish had trials with both clubs as an outside left. "But I had only one or two games – I didn't like soccer," he later recalled.

Fish returned to playing rugby and in 1896, while still only aged 17, he played five or six reserve team matches for Runcorn, who – like Warrington – had been founder members of the breakaway Northern Union, the body that would become the Rugby Football League. Runcorn, however, did not spot Fish's potential and let him slip through their fingers. It would prove to be a costly and perhaps even fatal mistake. Runcorn did not survive the Great War, although if Fish had been in their ranks for 13 seasons, pulling in spectators and helping them to win trophies, perhaps they would have done.

Fish continued to play for Lostock Gralam and the opening match of the 1898–99 season saw them at home to Warrington's 'A' team in the Lancashire Junior League. Now aged 19, Fish was fully grown and with a stocky, powerful build. He was 5 feet 7 inches tall and weighed 11 stone and, from his usual spot on the left wing, scored three tries in a beaten team.

Warrington 'A', who won 13-11, were managed by a larger-than-life character called James T. 'Tosh' Thorniley, a former Wirepullers forward. At more than 16 stones, Thorniley had been a formidable scrummager and was a man of substance. After the game, he approached Fish and asked him to sign for Warrington. Fish would not give a definite answer, but Thorniley knew that he had seen an outstanding talent in action, a player who was already equipped for the first team and one who would grace Wilderspool.

Lostock's next two games were away to Latchford Rangers and Warrington St Mary's, two of Warrington's leading junior teams, and Fish scored in both matches. Further talks were arranged between Fish and the Warrington committee; the club officials were determined to get their man.

When Fish entered the committee room on the evening of Wednesday 12 October 1898, he was faced with a table piled high with £5 in silver coins – about £1,000 in today's money – ready for him to take home. Fish, with his eyes glistening, said: "I did not know there was so much money in the world" and promptly signed the required forms.

The Northern Union was only three years old and still had a "working clause" to discourage idleness among its players. Under the working clause, if a player had not worked at least three days during the week he was not allowed to play for his club the following Saturday, unless he had a satisfactory explanation. The Northern Union even had a "Professionalism Committee" to implement the working clause and, occasionally, issue permits if a player had not worked enough days the previous week but had a satisfactory explanation, such as a doctor's certificate.

The Warrington committee, however, were not taking any chances and found Fish a job at Joseph Crosfield and Sons, the town's famous soap manufacturer, where he would work from six in the morning until six in the evening. His pay was 17s 10d per week (89 pence per week) – about £400 per week in today's money.

He would, of course, also be paid for playing, with winning money of 12s 6d (63p) and losing money of 10s (50p). Those figures would be about £250 and £200 today.

The *Warrington Guardian* reported Fish's signing as follows: "Possessed of a rare turn of speed, he makes the most of opportunities, and when he has become associated with the tricks of his captain, Fish should certainly prove an acquisition."

Warrington's captain, and best player, at the time was half-back James T. Bate who had the unusual nickname of 'Smack' because when he wanted the ball he would clap his hands once, making a smack sound. On Saturday 15 October 1898 – three days after Fish had signed for Warrington – he and Smack Bate lined up in the side to face Barrow in a friendly at Wilderspool and it did not take the winger long to open his account. The *Warrington Guardian* said that: "After Bate had experienced hard luck, he initiated a round of passing which terminated in Fish scoring a brilliant try." Warrington went on to win 10–5 in front of a crowd of about 3,000.

Fish made his competitive debut on a wretchedly wet afternoon at Rochdale one week later when the Wirepullers won 3–2. His competitive home debut – and his first official try – followed seven days later against Tyldesley, who were then known as the 'Mighty Bongers'. Warrington won 21–4. The *Warrington Guardian* reported Fish's try as follows: "Bate put the crowd in a good humour with a skilful movement, and Fish was hauled down inches from the corner flag. The spectators, however, had not long to wait, for the ball was whipped out to the open by Ashurst, and Fish raced through the opposing backs and scored."

Remarkably for the Warrington committee, lightning was about to strike twice in the same place. In November 1898 they signed another 19-year-old winger, a local lad by the name of Elliot Harris, this time

5

from the Latchford Rangers junior club, and he would prove to be almost as good as Fish himself.

By the end of the season Fish and Harris were the joint top try scorers, with 10 each, in all competitions. Harris, however, scored the bulk of his tries in friendly matches, leaving Fish to be the club's official leading try scorer, with eight, and points scorer, with 24.

Against Stockport in December, Fish scored the quickest try in his career, almost straight from the kick-off. The *Warrington Guardian* described the action: "Bate won the toss and Saville kicked off, and before the game had been fairly commenced Isherwood had a flying kick which Granger failed to hold, and Fish following up, picked up and ran round the posts, Holcroft kicking an easy goal."

Sometimes, Smack Bate would create his tries for him, but Fish was just as capable of creating tries for himself and his team-mates. At Wigan in January, Fish launched what would now be called an up-and-under. John Winstanley, the Wigan full-back, failed to collect it and Fish raced up, grabbed the ball and cantered over the line for an easy try.

One week later, however, he suffered a badly-bruised shoulder while scoring a try in the corner against Leigh and more trouble was on its way. Fish did not turn up for work in the week beginning Monday, 6 March and so was not allowed to play the following weekend. The Warrington committee decided to get tough and suspended him for two weeks. The *Warrington Examiner* newspaper urged Fish to back down: "If he returns to work and behaves himself, it is probable that he will be reinstated before the end of his sentence. I hope he will be sensible."

But Fish did not return to work and the suspension was extended to six weeks. In another editorial, the *Examiner* said that Fish had a "distaste for work" – although, perhaps he just had a distaste for 12-hour shifts at Crosfield's. Fish returned home to Lostock Gralam and, during the summer, found work with a firm that was sinking wells at Tarporley. It seemed that his Warrington career could be over before it had really begun.

Without Fish, Warrington won their Challenge Cup first round tie at home to Barrow before losing 14–0 at Oldham in a blizzard. The league campaign in the Lancashire Senior Competition had been a disappointment too, with more defeats – 14 – than victories – 11 – and more points conceded – 217 – than scored – 134.

However, it had been an historic season too because Warrington had moved to Wilderspool Stadium, which would become their home for the next 105 years. In truth, the club had not moved far – about 100 yards – so that the houses could be built in what is now Fletcher Street, but it was here that they would put down roots and find fame.

Warrington 8 Leigh 10. 9 September 1899. Back: D. Morrison (with hat), J. Taylor, A. Boardman; middle: J. Bate, J. Fairhurst, J. Hallam, W. Townend, J. Swift, J. Sudlow; sitting: E. Harris, A. Siddall, J. Ashurst, Naylor, J. Scholtze; kneeling: J. Duckworth, J. Fish, E. Jones (in jacket).

Swinton were the first visitors to the new Wilderspool on Saturday 3 September, for a match that ended in a 3–3 draw with Warrington stand-off Robert 'Bob' Bate – Smack's younger brother – scoring the first try on the new ground. The season also saw John 'Jack' Hallam make his first appearance at full-back, a position he would make his own for the next seven seasons.

Over the summer, Fish and the Warrington committee patched up their differences and the committee found their star winger a new job in the town at Rylands Brothers, the wire makers, where he was employed wheeling five hundredweights of wire away as it left the red-hot ovens. It was arduous work; Fish quickly complained about it and so another job was found, this time as a gas range fitter at the Fletcher Russells factory close to Wilderspool. This was Fish's job for the rest of his working life.

While Fish and the committee had been at loggerheads the townspeople were divided as well – over a 9 feet 6 inches tall bronze statue of Oliver Cromwell. The statue had been donated by Frederick Monks, a prominent civic figure and non-conformist, who had already presented the corporation with its impressive Town Hall gates.

A petition against the statue was signed by 2,121 Roman Catholic clergy and people of Warrington. It read: "We, the undersigned Catholic clergy and people of Warrington, have heard with very deep regret that the Town Council has accepted on behalf of the town a statue of Oliver Cromwell. We are pained to find that the Council could so far disregard the well-known sentiments of so large a number of those whom they represent, and with whose interests they have been entrusted. We hereby most strongly and indignantly protest against the erection of the statue on any public site or in any place belonging to the town. If not an eyesore, it would certainly be a daily heartsore in our midst.

"The evil that men do lives after them; and we could regard the erection of the statute only as an outrage on our feelings, calculated to awaken anew; and to perpetuate in our minds the bitter remembrance of the wrongs wrought by Cromwell – a remembrance which all his greatness, and the lapse of 250 years have not been able to efface.

"We conclude by earnestly hoping that when so much is being said about the peace of nations nothing will be done which is calculated to disturb the peaceful relations at present existing between the citizens of our town."

The petition, however, was ignored and the statue – to mark the 300th anniversary of Cromwell's birth – was erected at Bridge Foot and unveiled later in the year. Generations of Warrington supporters would pass it as they walked from the town centre to Wilderspool to watch the Wirepullers in action.

2. Five tries in a match

"My swerving and side-stepping came in useful"

Warrington supporters soon fell in love with Jack Fish. Even his name seemed to be just right and have a certain magic about it. On two occasions during the 1899–1900 season the initials of the four players in the threequarter line even spelt it out for all to see.

The first was on Saturday 27 January 1900 when Warrington were at home to Runcorn, Fish's home town team, and the threequarter line was Fish, Isherwood, Smith and Harris. Three weeks later, at Widnes, the quartet was Fish, Isherwood, Smith and Hockenhull. Unfortunately, Warrington lost both games, but the team was improving.

In August 1899, the committee had signed two centres, to try to get the best out of Fish and Harris. Welshman Evan Thomas Jones, a former Cardiff rugby union player, was signed from Huddersfield where he had been based for the previous two seasons while D.F. Mereweather was snapped up from the Bristol rugby union club, having previously played for Devonport Albion.

A crowd of 3,000 turned out at Wilderspool one Tuesday evening to watch them in their first practice match. Mereweather scored a try while Jones kicked a drop-goal. Frank Jewkes, a well-known local association footballer, also switched codes and started playing on the wing for the 'A' team.

Fish, of course, was still going to be the star of the show and against Leigh at Wilderspool in September he added a new string to his bow by kicking his first goal for the club. The conversion gave Warrington an 8–2 half-time lead before, in the second half, he went off with a leg injury and Harris was carried off. This gave Leigh a two-man advantage and helped them to win 10-8.

Fish missed the next five games and was eased back into action with an appearance for the 'A' team against Wigan 'A' when he signalled his return to fitness with his first hat-trick in primrose and blue. His first hat-trick for the first team followed at Leigh in December, but that was only the start.

Warrington were expected to beat Goole at Wilderspool in the second round of the Challenge Cup on Saturday 24 March, but Fish made sure that the afternoon would go down in the record books by becoming the first Warrington player to score five tries in a match. He also kicked seven goals, another club record, from nine attempts to finish with a Northern Union record 29 points in Warrington's 44–0 victory. Match reports of the time said that Fish was "here, there and everywhere".

Goole had beaten another Yorkshire team, Heckmondwike, in the first round and knew that if they won at Wilderspool there was every chance they would travel to Hull KR for a money-spinning derby match in the third round because the draw had already been made.

The "giddy Goolians" – as one writer described them – were only worried about one Warrington player, Jack Fish, whose fame had already spread to the East Riding of Yorkshire. Their fears turned into a grim reality. Early on, after a good run, Fish kicked the ball across to his waiting forward John Eden, who knocked on under the posts when it looked easier to score. No matter. After 15 minutes, Fish dodged down the left and, this time, passed to Eden, who scored near the corner. Fish kicked a superb conversion to put Warrington 5–0 ahead.

Approaching half-time, Fish received a pass from centre Danny Isherwood and raced behind the posts for the second Wire try and added the goal himself to make the score 10–0 at the break. In the second half, Warrington played with the wind and cut loose. Fish collected a pass from Eden to run in for the third try and again added the goal. Isherwood and forward Dave Morrison scored the next two tries and two more Fish goals made it 25–0.

Winger Freddie Moores scored the sixth try and although Fish missed the kick, he improved his own score minutes later to stretch Warrington's lead to 33–0. Two more Fish tries followed, after passes by J Taylor and Smack Bate, before centre Tom Hockenhull added the 10th Warrington try and Fish completed the scoring with his seventh goal.

Following this remarkable and record-breaking performance, Fish received a 20 per cent pay rise, worth about £50 per week in today's money, from the committee. His winning pay and losing pay was increased by 2s 6d per game with his winning pay going up from 12s 6d (63p) to 15s (75p) and his losing pay increasing from 10s (50p) to 12s 6d (63p). In modern terms, his winning pay was now £300 per match while his losing pay was £250. He proved to be worth every penny.

Warrington's reward for their victory over Goole was a trip to Rochdale, who had beaten Hull KR, in the third round. Rochdale's pitch was hidden under a two-inch layer of mud, topped with a scattering of sawdust – conditions which were very much against the Wire. Still the game seemed to be headed for a 0–0 draw until a mistake by Jack Hallam, Warrington's otherwise outstanding full-back, allowed Rochdale to score a try. Fish made one brilliant run near the end, but was slowed down by the mud and tackled.

Warrington were out of the cup and, except for three friendly matches, their season was over. Fish and Morrison, Warrington's best back and best forward, were selected for the 'Rest of League' team to take on Runcorn, the winners of the Lancashire Senior Competition, at Runcorn on Saturday 21 April, in a special challenge match.

Fish's first full season with the club had been a personal triumph. He was the leading try scorer and leading goalkicker and, aged just 21, his best years were still to come. His natural speed and ability to stop dead in his tracks and start off again almost immediately served him well, but to avoid heavy tackles he also worked on his swerve and side-step.

"To put it frankly," he admitted in an interview in 1936, "I was a bit timid of the bump, and I used to jib a bit when I saw the tackle coming. And as I jibbed I found that I was frequently beating a man. So I set out to learn how to swerve, and that is what I did.

"I put a few sticks in a row in the ground leaving a few yards between them and I ran as hard as I could towards them swerving past one and then another. As I progressed I was able to narrow the gaps between the sticks until instead of a few yards there was no more than a few feet separating them. Then when I could go in between them without slackening my pace a lot I was satisfied.

"I used to stab my left heel into the ground and throw myself back, and then I would move inside on to my right foot and be off again. My swerving and side-stepping came in useful."

It was only a matter of time before Fish's talents were recognised by his county, Lancashire, and he took part in a trial match at St Helens' Knowsley Road ground on Wednesday 3 October 1900. He scored a try and kicked two goals. He played for the Probables against the Possibles and immediately won selection for the county side.

He was chosen for the Lancashire team to play Cumberland at Workington on Saturday 20 October in the County Championship. To make sure that the players were in the best possible condition, the team travelled the day before and reaped the benefit with a 21–2 win.

Oldham winger Sam Williams took the scoring honours with three tries, but Fish kicked three goals and was looking forward to Lancashire's next match, the big one, against Yorkshire at Rochdale on Saturday 3 November.

Surprisingly, Fish was dropped by the county committee and replaced by a centre, Bob Valentine, amid suggestions that picking the better-known Swinton player might boost the attendance for the match. The snub was good news for Warrington on two fronts. First, Fish was now available to play against Widnes at Wilderspool in the South West Lancashire Cup tie that was being played on the same day as the county match. Secondly, he now had something to prove to the county selectors.

Against Widnes he raced in for a hat-trick of tries in a performance which saw him described as the "artful dodger" by the *Warrington Guardian*, after the Charles Dickens character in *Oliver Twist*. He scored another try against St Helens in the next round as Warrington booked their place in the final against Leigh.

Warrington were on the up and added another exciting talent to their ranks at the end of October when a 19-year-old local lad, George Dickenson, made his debut. The four members of Warrington's first great threequarter line – Fish, Isherwood, Dickenson and Harris – were now in the team and lined up as a unit together for the first time against Runcorn at Wilderspool on Boxing Day 1900.

Over the next five years they would become known as the 'Aristocratic Four' and their play was described as "poetry in motion". All four won representative honours.

The complete draw for the Challenge Cup was made before the competition started and so Warrington knew in January that if they could beat Leeds at Headingley in the first round they would then be faced with three home ties up to the semi-final.

This seemed like a golden opportunity to reach the final and so the committee decided to "stiffen the scrimmage" before the Challenge Cup transfer deadline on 1 February.

Warrington suffered an embarrassing league defeat at Millom on 19 January – they lost 3–2 – but the journey to Cumberland was not entirely wasted as the committee signed two big forwards from the Askham club: Tom Fell and Jim Edmondson, who weighed 13 stone 2 pounds and 13 stone 1 pound respectively. Both made their debuts in a 2–2 draw against Barrow at Wilderspool the following week and so were settled into the team by the time the Challenge Cup kicked off on the first Saturday in March.

The committee made a significant change at stand-off for the first cup game, dropping the captain, Smack Bate, and replacing him with his brother, Bob, and the switch paid off as Warrington produced one of their best performances of the season to win 19–0 at Headingley. Smack never played for Warrington again and retired shortly afterwards. He was replaced as captain by Danny Isherwood.

Two special trains had left Warrington for Leeds, with supporters paying return fares of 3s. Among them were the Warrington Male Voice Choir who gave the team vocal support from the stand as Jack Fish scored two tries and kicked two goals.

Heckmondwike, the Yorkshire Second Division leaders, travelled to Wilderspool for the second round tie one week later and were duly despatched 19–2. Jack Fish claimed a hat-trick.

Another Yorkshire team, Leeds Parish Church, were at Wilderspool in the third round, but with Bob Bate once again outstanding Warrington won 11–0. Fish hit the post twice with kicks, once when trying to convert his own try and once with a penalty, but – with the last kick of the match – he converted an Elliot Harris try to bring up 100 points for the season.

Bradford, the Yorkshire champions, were at Wilderspool in the fourth round for a match that attracted a 10,000 crowd, including 1,500 from Yorkshire. Bradford were almost a stone per man heavier and, shortly before kick-off, Warrington lost full-back Jack Hallam with an ankle injury.

He was replaced with Ernest Ratcliffe, an 'A' team threequarter, who rose to the occasion magnificently and kicked a goal from the touchline to convert Jack Fish's opening try. Warrington held on to win 10–8, although Bradford missed a late conversion attempt that would have levelled the scores and forced a replay.

All the while, according to the 1901 Census, Fish was working as a gas range fitter and lodging at 10 Sparling Street, Latchford, with a blacksmith, Alfred Mather, his wife, Elizabeth and their four children John aged 7, Harold, 6, Alsie, 3, and baby Alfred of just two weeks. As a special treat, young Harold was allowed to carry 'Uncle Jack's' boots to matches, a tale he would proudly tell and retell many times in later life – and he lived to the grand old age of 97.

Fish, however, was in love and on Thursday 4 April 1901, aged 22, he got married to his 21-year-old sweetheart Fanny Quarmby at St James' Church. His best man was local rugby player Ernie Jordan, who joined Fish in the Warrington team in October 1903. He made 81 appearances and scored 17 tries for the club. Fish returned the compliment a few years later, by acting as the best man when Jordan himself got married.

It was to be the briefest of honeymoons because Fish played in a friendly against Bradford side Manningham at Wilderspool two days later; he scored two tries and kicked three goals in a 24–0 victory. A ground collection was held for supporters to donate and wish the new Mr and Mrs Fish a happy married life in their new home, in Prince Street in Warrington.

Yet another Yorkshire team, Castleford, awaited Warrington in the Challenge Cup semi-final at Broughton and they decided to detail two players to mark Jack Fish. The plan was fine in theory, but did not work in practice because Fish scored three tries, ran the length of the field to complete his hat-trick, and kicked two goals. He had now scored tries and kicked goals in every round: 10 tries and eight goals in all.

Warrington decided not to do any special training for the final, believing that the usual Tuesday and Friday sessions would be enough to keep them fit. The final, like Warrington's first round tie, was at Headingley and the Wirepullers were up against the Gallant Youths of Batley who had won the competition in 1897 and 1898. The teams lined up as follows:

13

Batley: Garner, Davies, Fitzgerald, Goodall, Auty, Oakley, Midgley, Fisher, Judge, Rodgers, Stubley, Spurr, Maine, Fozzard, Hollingworth.
Warrington: Hallam, Fish, Isherwood, Dickenson, Harris, Bate, Duckworth, Boardman, Fell, Edmondson, Scholtze, Eden, Cunningham, Morrison, Swift.
Referee: J. Kidd (Millom)

The average age of the Warrington side was 24 and, on the big day and in front of a then record 29,000-plus crowd, they froze, with Fish never getting a chance to show his worth. Fish, himself, missed an early penalty goal attempt from the touchline before Batley's Wattie Davies scored the opening try following a bad pass from Danny Isherwood to George Dickenson that went to ground. Wilf Auty scored the second Batley try in the corner after Dickenson had misfielded and then seen his clearing kick charged down.

Wattie Davies missed both kicks, but Batley were still 6-0 ahead approaching half-time when Jack Fish and Wilf Auty were cautioned by the referee for fighting. George Maine, the Batley forward, was sent off in the second half for rough play − he was later suspended until 1 December − but, even with 14 men, Batley remained the better team. They held on to win 6-0 and claim the Challenge Cup for the third and, to date, final time.

The gate receipts for the Final were £1,644, but Warrington and Batley only received £50 each. On hearing this, the Warrington committee immediately asked the Northern Union to make a charitable donation to Warrington Infirmary.

Two days after the Challenge Cup Final, Warrington faced Leigh in the South West Lancashire Cup Final at Springfield Park, Wigan, playing for the same trophy they had won as the South West Lancashire and Border Towns Cup in 1886. In front of a 6,000 crowd, the game finished scoreless and it was too dark for any extra time to be played.

A replay was arranged for the following day at Widnes. However, Harry Ashton, the Warrington secretary, sent Leigh a telegram saying they did not have enough fit players left to raise a team. Leigh still turned up for the replay and waited for two hours before returning home and were later awarded the cup by default.

During the 1900–01 season, Fish had become the first Warrington player to score 100 points in a season − he finished the campaign with 118 − and, more impressively, the first Wirepuller to score 20 tries in a campaign. He finished with 22, including 14 in the two cup competitions. He was also the club's leading goalkicker, with 26. Throughout the Northern Union, only one player, Oldham's Sam Williams, scored more points than him.

People, including rugby players, were smaller 100 years ago and so none of the Warrington team was 6 feet tall or weighed 14 stones −

dimensions which are almost obligatory today. The following list was published in March 1901.

Backs

Jack Hallam	5ft 7in	12st 7lb
Jack Fish	5ft 7in	11st 8lb
Danny Isherwood	5ft 7in	11st 1lb
George Dickenson	5ft 9in	11st 2lb
Elliot Harris	5ft 7in	12st 8lb
Bob Bate	5ft 8in	10st 12lb
Jack Duckworth	5ft 6in	10st 10lb
Tom Hockenhull	5ft 7in	11st 2lb

Forwards

Alf Boardman	5ft 11in	13st 10lb
Tom Fell	5ft 9in	13st
Jim Edmondson	5ft 10in	12st 8lb
John Eden	5ft 8in	12st 6lb
D Mereweather	5ft 7in	12st 8lb
J Scholtze	5ft 11in	12st 10lb
J Swift	5ft 7in	13st 2lb
J Cunningham	5ft 9in	12st 7lb
Dave Morrison	5ft 10in	12st 8lb

Warrington at Barrow in 1901: Back: D. Morrison, J. Hallam, W. Swift, J. Jolley, G. Dickenson, J. Cunningham; middle: F. Swift, T. Hockenhull, D. Isherwood, J. Eden, A. Scholtze, A. Boardman; sitting: J. Duckworth, J. Fish, A Burgess.

Warrington 1901–02: Back: Morrison, Fish, Isherwood, Harris, Dickenson, Hallam, Burgess, Boardman; middle: Cunningham, F. Swift, Fell, T.W. Swift, Eden, Jolley, Edmondson; front: Allen, Hockenhull.

3. The worst spectators in England

"When I was at my best I was round about an 11 seconds man"

Jack Fish and Warrington warmed up for the 1901–02 season by travelling to County Durham to play South Shields on Wednesday 4 September with a 6pm kick-off. The North East club had resigned from the Rugby Football Union and joined the Northern Union at the end of the previous season and this was Warrington's way of showing their support. In front of 2,000 spectators, the Wirepullers won 14–7 with Fish, almost inevitably, scoring three tries and kicking a goal. Elliot Harris scored the other Warrington try.

The victory put Warrington in good heart for the first game of the season three days later, against Batley at Wilderspool, in a repeat of April's Challenge Cup final. Warrington won 15–3 – by five tries to one – but that only tells half of the story.

The game was still in the first half when Wattie Davies, Batley's Welsh winger, and Arthur Burgess, the Warrington scrum-half, were sent off for fighting. Burgess left the field quietly, but Davies jumped over the fence into the 5,000-strong crowd and punched Warrington supporter William Brown, giving him a black eye.

Davies was pulled out of the crowd by police officers and led away to the changing rooms. Brown, with the support of the Warrington committee, took legal action against the Welshman, who filed a counter-claim. Davies appeared at Warrington County Borough Police Court on Friday, 20 September, where he agreed to apologise to all concerned in return for all charges being dropped.

His apology appeared in local newspapers as follows: "To Mr William Brown, of 49, Hopwood Street, Warrington and to the committee and members of Warrington Football Club.

"I, the undersigned Wharton Davies of Batley, Yorkshire, do hereby express my regret to you for my conduct on the Football Ground at Warrington on the 7th of September instant in striking one of your spectators, the said William Brown, and I promise that the same shall not occur again.

"Dated this 20th day of September, 1901. WHARTON DAVIES."

Safely back in Batley, however, Davies gave a somewhat different version of events in a letter to the *Yorkshire Evening Post*, which was published on Saturday 21 September as follows: "The game was a very keen one, as the Warringtonians were evidently bent on taking their revenge for their cup defeat in April of this year. Burgess, one of the Warrington half backs, and I chanced to incur the displeasure of the referee, with the result that we got sent off the field.

"As I walked down the touchline I was struck by a spectator, and I then jumped over the rails and retaliated, but the police soon interfered, and very little came of it. Today (Friday) I had to appear in answer to the summons, and I was persuaded to apologise so that the matter might be hushed up in the interests of sport, with the result that, although I was the assaulted party, I have to practically acknowledge that I was the guilty party.

"Instead of hushing things up, the Warrington committee have, despite the agreement we came to, given the affair as much publicity as they possibly could. A friend of mine in Warrington advised me to come to some agreement instead of taking the case to court. As I had no witnesses myself – we (Batley) having no spectators with us – I thought the best thing I could do in the case was to, if possible, come to some terms, which I was persuaded to do to my sorrow. I am writing this to warn all clubs in Yorkshire who are desirous of taking care of their players, to keep a good guard over them, as the Warrington spectators are the worst spectators in England."

Warrington refuted his allegations with their own statement from solicitors Davies and Forshaw: "We are instructed by the committee of the Warrington Rugby Football Club to say that the statements contained therein are grossly misleading. It is quite untrue that Davies was struck by a spectator whilst walking down the touchline. He was the aggressor, and was so violent that he had to be removed by the police to the pavilion and afterwards to the dressing room. The summons which he states was taken out by him was only taken out after he had been served with a summons for assaulting a spectator named Brown, and was taken out by his solicitor simply as a matter of form, but Davies was struck neither on nor off the field of play.

"It was at the earnest request of Davies and his solicitor that the complainant and the committee withdrew the summons, upon Davies agreeing to apologise to the complainant and the committee, and he agreed to the apology being published in the Warrington papers and paid all the costs of the prosecution. This is all the publicity the Warrington committee have given to this unpleasant incident.

"Davies stated in his letter that 'he was persuaded to come to terms to his sorrow.' No pressure was brought to bear upon him to come to terms by ourselves or our clients, as he was represented by his solicitor, who advised him to settle the matter as stated in order to avoid a conviction being recorded against him, thereby bringing the Batley club into bad repute. The rest of Davies' letter is ridiculous, and further comment is needless."

The Northern Union, supported by the referee and a touch judge, believed Warrington more than Davies and suspended the Welshman for two months. Burgess only received a one-month ban.

Fish would have followed this episode with a mixture of amusement and indignation, but on Saturday 21 September he had other things on his mind as his wife, Fanny, gave birth at home at Prince Street to a baby girl called Edith. Being a Saturday, of course, he still played for Warrington away to Broughton Rangers that afternoon.

It was a magnificent match, played before a crowd of 9,000. Just before half-time Fish was carried off with a leg injury, but he was able to resume playing at the start of the second half. Fully recovered, he sprinted clear of the Broughton defence to touch down a kick to the corner. Jack Hallam failed with the conversion attempt but later added a long-range penalty to make the score 5–3. A minute from time, however, Broughton winger Arthur Widdeson picked up a loose ball, eluded Elliot Harris and scored a try to condemn Warrington to a dramatic 6–5 defeat.

Warrington's two home games in October were equally memorable, although for very different reasons. On Saturday 12 October, the committee officially opened a brick-built pavilion, complete with changing rooms and baths. Previously, from the formation of the Warrington club in 1876, the players had got changed in pubs, including the Patten Arms and the White Hart, and then walked to the ground ready for kick-off. Swinton were the visitors and somewhat spoiled the party by winning 3–0, but the pavilion, which cost £295, about £20,000 in today's money, was hailed as a big success. Admission prices had been raised to 6d, in line with Northern Union rules, and 9d on the stand side, to help pay for the pavilion.

Seven days later, Fish scored one of the finest tries of his career to seal a 15–5 victory over a strong Oldham side. At the start of the second half, Warrington were leading 12–3, but were under huge pressure on their own line at the Railway End of the ground.

Fish intercepted a pass meant for Oldham winger Viv Huzzey, who had won five caps for the Wales rugby union team before going north and was one of the fastest men in the game. Fish easily beat Dixon, the Oldham full-back, but Huzzey was right behind him, matching him stride for stride. Huzzey even seemed to be scraping at Fish's jersey, with Fish instinctively drawing himself in each time to stay inches ahead. Fish won the race to seal the victory and Huzzey was the first to congratulate him while a crowd of 7,000 cheered for several minutes.

By the end of 1901, Warrington had beaten the Challenge Cup holders, Batley, the Yorkshire League champions, Bradford, the Cheshire champions, Runcorn, and the Lancashire League champions, Oldham. The 10–3 victory over Runcorn was their first over the Linnets since 1885 – 16 years earlier – after a dreadful run made up of 15 defeats and two draws.

19

Warrington lost 19–8 to Bradford at Wilderspool on New Year's Day, but not before Fish scored what he later believed to be the best try of his entire career. He swerved and side-stepped past practically the whole Bradford team, leaving a trail of baffled opponents behind him, and finished with a try near the posts after a run which covered nearly the length of the field.

Warrington eventually finished a disappointing seventh out of the 14 teams in the Northern League. But their results in the subsidiary South West Lancashire League remained impressive and with seven wins and a draw from their 10 matches Warrington finished joint top with Widnes. So it was decided that a play-off between the two would be held at Runcorn's Canal Street ground on the evening of Tuesday 29 April to determine the champions. A crowd of 5,000 turned out to watch the action.

Widnes struck first, with a Lally drop-goal from the base of a scrum giving them a 2–0 lead. A Jack Fish penalty goal equalised the scores before he then called a mark and kicked another goal from the half-way line to make the half-time score 4–2. After the interval, scrum-half Arthur Burgess made a break and passed to centre George Dickenson who found Fish in support. The winger did the rest to score a magnificent try behind the posts.

Inexplicably, Fish then missed the conversion and Warrington were reduced to 14 men when forward Harry Forster was sent off for a late tackle but, with Fish and Elliot Harris making key marks, the Wirepullers held on to win 14–7. Dave Morrison had been Warrington's best forward, and played his best game for the club.

Fish, who had taken over as captain from the injured Danny Isherwood in February, received the cup and the team received their medals. A large crowd was waiting for the players when they arrived back in Warrington and, accompanied by the Borough Band, they paraded through several streets, with Fish showing off the cup from the top of a wagonette. He had won his first trophy, and as captain too, and although it was only the South West Lancashire League it was a start. Another award came Fish's way in May when he was presented with his Lancashire cap, having played in all four of their matches during the season, scoring five tries.

May 1902 also saw Warrington make another significant signing when they recruited the promising stand-off Ernie Brookes, aged 18, from the Bewsey junior club. Brookes went on to make 297 appearances for the first team and scored 81 tries. Years later, he would joke that his modest signing-on fee had been a pat on the back, a bottle of pop and a cigar – and he didn't even smoke.

During the summer, Fish put his famous sprinting powers to the test and came through with flying colours. The occasion was Warrington

Football Club's 18th annual athletic festival and gala – an important fund-raising event in the club's early years – at Wilderspool on Bank Holiday Monday 4 August 1902.

Fish entered the 100 yards and 220 yards sprint handicap races and his presence, combined with brilliant sunshine, helped to attract a record crowd of 8,000. He was given a seven-and-a-half yards start by the handicapper in the 100 yards sprint and was one of 11 heat winners. He won his second round race as well and, in the final, he won by a foot from the Manchester sprinter W. Jervis, who had a slightly more generous handicap of eight yards. Fish's time was 10 seconds dead and his prize for winning the blue riband event was the best one of the day, a magnificent carved oak bracket chime clock worth £10, about £800 in today's money.

In the 220 yards event, Fish was given a 14 yards start by the handicapper and again won his heat to join seven other heat winners in the final. In the final itself, he romped home by two yards ahead of the London athlete A.E. Hare, whose handicap was a slightly tougher 10 yards, in a time of 22 seconds.

To complete a good afternoon for Warrington players, and to show what natural athletes they were, team-mate Elliot Harris won the 440 yards title. Operating with a 20-yard start, Harris won his heat and, in the final, finished two yards clear of the field in a time of 49.3 seconds.

After finishing the previous season on a high, and with wingers Fish and Harris in tip-top condition, the Warrington supporters were looking forward to a successful 1902–03 campaign. What they got was an inconsistent one. The Wirepullers won 14 games, lost 14 games and drew seven. At least it was symmetrical.

Warrington's problems began from day one when full-back Jack Hallam refused to play after failing to agree terms with the committee. This newspaper profile of the player had appeared the previous season and showed what an outstanding 'custodian' he was.

"Few players in the Northern Union have earned so much genuine respect of football enthusiasts as John Hallam, the sturdy full-back of the Warrington club. Unassuming, straight-forward, honest in every detail, Hallam has since he took up the post which Boscow, the old Warrington back, was compelled by weight of years to relinquish, won for himself a warm place among the admirers of the handling code. It was the proud boast of the Warrington club at one period that all their players were born within the borough. The exigencies of time, however, caused the executive to look afield for players to fill the places which were rapidly being vacated by such men as Turner, Dillon, Povey, Speakman, Gilbert, Barnes and Buxton. But one must not run away with the impression that Hallam was sought for outside.

WARRINGTON'S FULL-BACK.

J. HALLAM.

Jack Hallam (Courtesy Robert Gate)

"Although not a native, he is practically a Warrington man. He was born in 1876 at Stoke-on-Trent, and, living in such a hotbed of Association football, Hallam's early inclinations were naturally towards the dribbling game. As a schoolboy Hallam was one of the most promising inside rights in the Potteries. However, on his parents removing to Huddersfield, he had to forego all ideas of following up Association, and the only sport with which he became identified in the Yorkshire town was cricket. That Hallam benefited here to a great extent is certain, for he received valuable tuition from no less a celebrity than George Henry Hirst, and is now regarded as one of the foremost cricketers in the Warrington district, being connected with the premier club.

"After staying for two seasons at Huddersfield, the Hallam family were drafted to Warrington, and Rugby being the dominating game, Hallam soon became associated with Latchford Rangers, then regarded as the leading junior team for miles around. He soon accustomed himself to the game, and for two seasons exhibited a defence which could not escape the keen eyes of Warrington followers of the game in general. Directly Latchford won the junior championship of the County Palatine, Hallam was secured by Warrington. Whilst playing with the Rangers he had such confreres as Harris, Hockenhull, Boardman and R. Bate, all of whom are at the present time doing good work for the premier club. It was in 1895 that Hallam got his first real chance with Warrington. He was deputed to play with the 'A' team against Widnes 'A', and such was his display that his claims could not be overlooked. Singular to relate in the afternoon, after playing against Widnes, he

22

took the field in the senior team for the first time and played a defensive game, which was the opening to a highly successful career.

"The retirement of Boscow was Hallam's opportunity, and he has been the recognized back since that period. Hallam has not yet won honours as a county player, but is still hopeful that they will yet come his way. He has figured repeatedly on the reserve, but so consistent has been the form of the original selections that his services have not been requisitioned. He is an ideal back, standing 5 feet 8 inches height and scaling 12 stone 8 pounds. He has a powerful and judicious kick. He has displayed consistently good form throughout the present season and has been the hope and stay of the team when it has been in its tightest corners."

The Warrington committee, however, refused to give in to Hallam's wage demands and Hallam, in turn, refused to play. The committee selected Hallam's understudy, Tommy Knight, instead, even though he was an inferior player. The stalemate dragged on for three months. In October, Hallam started playing for his former club, Latchford Rangers, for free and helped them to defeat Widnes Rangers with his fine kicking and running.

Finally, after Warrington had suffered back-to-back defeats away to Hull Kingston Rovers and Hunslet in late November, the two sides came to an agreement and Hallam was welcomed back into the fold.

Warrington and their players were also experiencing problems with the Northern Union's working clause. Warrington were fined a nominal 10s 6d after centre George Dickenson was found to have broken the working clause by playing at Halifax in October. The player himself was banned for a month. The working clause also denied prop Alf Boardman an appearance for Lancashire against Cheshire in October. Boardman was also prevented from playing for Warrington against Leigh on the same day.

Jack Fish, too, fell foul of the Professional Committee and was not allowed to play for Warrington against Bradford in December despite presenting a doctor's certificate which claimed that he had not been fit to work, even though he was now fit to play.

The following month the Northern Counties Athletic Association banned Fish from competing in their events because he was deemed to be professional. Perhaps, as well, he had been successful and won too many of their races, pocketing a lot of prize money in the process.

Fish maintained that, at his peak, he could sprint 100 yards in 11 seconds, but felt that with proper training he would have got closer to 10 seconds: "When I played football and I was at my best I was round about an 11 seconds man," he said in an interview in 1936. "But I always reckoned that had I trained seriously for the track I should have got near to evens. I only went into proper training once, and that was when I had my £50-a-side match with 'Bucky' Green, of Wigan." [1]

In January 1903 Fish injured his left hand in the last few minutes of the league match against Batley. He fractured cartilage and suffered severe bruising to a finger. The injury ruled him out for a month and meant that he missed the Challenge Cup first-round tie at struggling St Helens, which Warrington lost 6–0.

Not for the first time that season, the Warrington forwards were outplayed while captain Danny Isherwood was the only back to do himself justice. The committee had gambled on playing George Dickenson, who had been suffering from flu, and the gamble backfired when the centre producing a subdued performance. To cap it all, stand-off Arthur Burgess arrived late, meaning that the kick-off had to be put back from 3.30pm to 3.45pm. Warrington were later fined 16s by the Northern Union for the late start.

When everyone was fit, Warrington's backs were among the best in the league and when winger Elliot Harris was picked for Lancashire against Cheshire in October it meant that all four of the 'Aristocratic Four' – Fish, Isherwood, Dickenson and Harris – had played for their county. Warrington's problems were with the forwards, so it was a real bonus when Arthur Naylor returned to the club in November after three years of service with the Grenadier Guards in South Africa, which earned him a campaign medal.

Still, Warrington supporters were critical of the committee for not signing new players, especially forwards, before the Challenge Cup deadline. In fact, the only major signing of the season came in March when the Wirepullers snapped up centre Richard Mahoney from Cardiff rugby union club's second team.

Mahoney, aged 20, was 5 feet 8 inches tall, weighed 10 stone 12 pounds, and was regarded as one of the best young centres in South Wales. He was chased by several Northern Union clubs. Harry Ashton, the Warrington secretary, travelled to South Wales to complete the deal. Mahoney made his Warrington debut for the 'A' team at Broughton the following week. His first team debut came the following season when he made 16 appearances without scoring a try and did not really make the grade.

Despite everything, Warrington achieved some outstanding results in the 1902–03 season, particularly against Halifax who went on to be the First Division champions. At Halifax in October, Warrington achieved a 2–2 draw in front of a crowd of 10,000 thanks to a drop-goal from Arthur Burgess.

---

[1] This occurred in 1905 and is covered in chapter 5.

The return fixture was at Wilderspool on Good Friday and attracted a crowd of 10,000 who paid ground record receipts of £257, at least £20,000 in today's money. If Halifax won they would be the champions. If Warrington won then Salford could still take the title for Lancashire. There was no score at half-time but, in the second half, stand-off Jack Duckworth kicked a drop-goal to win the match and bring back memories of Warrington's famous victory over Wakefield Trinity in January 1888. Halifax, however, still went on to take the title.

Despite this win it had been a disappointing season and certainly not good enough for the club members who were very critical of the committee at the annual meeting at the Working Men's club in Market Place in May. The members felt that the club had the best threequarter line in the Northern Union, but that the forwards were not good enough to supply them with the possession they needed.

Warrington finished eighth out of the 18 teams in the First Division while the 'A' team were third in the Lancashire Combination. For once, the try of the season was not scored by Jack Fish, but by George Dickenson, who dribbled the ball past three players to score against Broughton Rangers at Wilderspool in March.

As always, the season was not without its lighter moments, including the sending off of 'Little Tich' Edmunds, the 5 feet tall Warrington stand-off and possibly the smallest player in the club's history, after he "set about" the 6 feet tall St Helens forward Frank Lee during the match at Knowsley Road in October.

The report to the disciplinary committee took up the story: "The giant took the Lilliputian in his arms and shook him as he would a child, the Warringtonian the while making it as uncomfortable as possible for his captor. The referee intervened and the two were given marching orders. It must have been a pretty sight to see this ill-matched couple walking off the field side-by-side. Lee said he never felt so ashamed in his life, though he vowed he did no more than pick up his smaller antagonist. He lifted him, he said, because he could not find in his heart to do more." 'Little Tich' – named after the music hall comedian Harry Relph – was suspended for two weeks while Lee was banned for a month.

These, however, were turbulent times in Jack Fish's private life. At the start of 1903, his wife, Fanny, gave birth to their second child, another daughter, named Alice. But a few months later, on 27 June, their first child, Edith, died at home aged 21 months from bronchitis and convulsions. The couple lost two more children in infancy over the coming years; secret pain that most Warrington supporters never knew about but which bound them together.

Jack Fish, Jim Stuntz and Dan Frawley relaxing before a match.

Jack Fish and Dan Frawley smartly dressed on a night out.

4. Winning the Challenge Cup

"Fish went past him easily as if he were merely a dummy figure needing only to be avoided."

By the start of the 1903–04 season, Jack Fish had been at Warrington for five years and was already a legend. He had made more than 100 appearances, scoring 71 tries and kicking 77 goals. He was the fastest player the club had ever seen and had a remarkable ability to take awkward passes.

To reward his talents, the Warrington committee gave him £3 to sign for the new season and increased his pay again to 20 shillings (£1) win, lose or draw, which made him the club's highest-paid player. In modern terms, that would equate to a signing-on fee of £1,000 and a match fee of about £350.

Team-mate George Dickenson was also highly thought of. He received £4 to sign for the new season, £1 more than Fish, but his match fees were not so generous – 17s 6d (88p) for a win and 12s 6d (63p) for a defeat or a draw.

In rugby terms, Fish was a genius and the supporters' expectations of him were high, but he was also a maverick and matters came to a head in November 1903. Still only 24, Fish did not turn up for work in the week leading up to the home game against Oldham, which meant he was not allowed to play under the Northern Union's working clause. When they found out, the supporters were furious and the committee suspended him for two weeks.

The *Warrington Examiner* did not mince its words: "It is a great pity so fine a player does not recognise his responsibilities and give the club the service it is entitled to. I never knew the Warrington crowd to be more 'raw' than last Saturday when they found Fish absent, and lost the match for that reason. The opinion that he should be suspended was general and the committee have taken that unpleasant course. Fish will therefore not play until November 28th at Bradford. He has merited the punishment and I hope he will mend his ways, otherwise his popularity will soon wane. The crowd will not support a man who treats his club as Fish has done lately."

By the end of the season, however, all the unpleasantness had been forgotten as Fish, at his brilliant best, had helped Warrington reach their second Challenge Cup final and win the South West Lancashire League. For the Challenge Cup final at Salford, hundreds of Warrington fans wore copper and brass 'Fish' badges, made in the workshops of the town, during Warrington supporters' lunch hours.

On the eve of the season, Warrington signed two forwards to bolster their pack: Welshman George Thomas from Newport and

27

Cheshire county scrummager Tom Cook from Birkenhead. When Thomas arrived at the club, some members of the committee questioned his small stature for a forward, he was only 5 feet 8 inches tall and weighed just 12 stone 11 pounds. Thomas replied: "Good stuff lies in little room." And so it would prove, although there were newspaper suggestions during the season that he should be played at stand-off rather than in the pack because of his pace and rugby skills. In October, Cook enlisted with the Scottish Fusiliers, but almost immediately regretted it and changed his mind.

One week before the season started winger Elliot Harris broke his collarbone in a practice match, an injury that would keep him out of the first team for two months. The unfortunate Harris broke his collarbone again, at Bradford in November, but took consolation from the fact that he would be fit again for the Challenge Cup, the game's glamour competition.

Warrington started the season, for the first time in their history, with two Welsh half-backs, stand-off 'Little Tich' Edmunds and scrum-half Dai Davies. By the end of the campaign, however, Edmunds had been replaced by Tom Hockenhull and transferred to Hull.

In October, Fish took part in possibly the most bizarre game of his entire career, a Lancashire county trial match between the Probables and the Possibles at Wilderspool on a Monday afternoon. It was played as a 12-a-side rather than a 15-a-side contest, with each side having six forwards but only three threequarters. To add to the surreal nature of the occasion, Fish also managed to play and score for both teams.

Roared on by 3,000 supporters, Fish scored two tries and kicked three goals in the first half as the Probables built up a 28–0 lead by half-time. During the interval, because the match was so one-sided, the selection committee instructed the backs to change sides, which allowed Fish to score a try and kick a goal for the Possibles as they closed the gap to 31–8 by the final whistle.

After the match, the committee met in the Patten Arms and picked the Lancashire team to play Cheshire. Fish, of course, was included with centre George Dickenson and prop Alf Boardman named as reserves. Boardman was awarded his county cap in February. The game against Cheshire, also 12-a-side, was staged at Broughton. Fish scored two tries, created two more and thrilled the 3,000-strong crowd with some brilliant runs down the touchline as Lancashire won 26–5.

Fish, it seemed, could do no wrong. Two weeks later, however, he failed to show up for work, was unable to play against Oldham and was suspended for two weeks. He started to rebuild his reputation almost immediately. Playing for Lancashire against Northumberland and Durham at South Shields, he kicked four goals and ran in three tries, one a length-of-the-field spectacular, as Lancashire won 42–0.

28

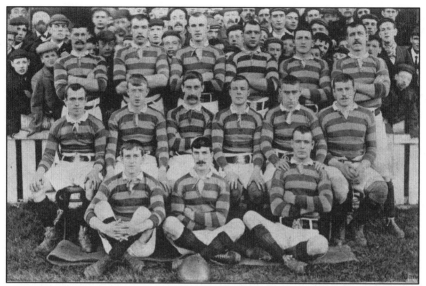

Warrington team in 1904: Back: A. Naylor, J. Preston, J. Belton, F. Shugars, G. Thomas, J. Jolley; sitting: C. Short, G. Dickenson, J. Hallam, D. Isherwood, J. Fish, A. Boardman; kneeling: D. Davies, T. Hockenhull, T. Cook.

At Salford, on Boxing Day, he scored one of the best tries of his career to give Warrington their first win at The Willows in front of a 10,000-strong holiday crowd. Gathering the ball near his own line, he twisted and swerved past a couple of players before bluffing the great James Lomas, the game's first £100 signing, on his way to touching down. Fish also scored another try and kicked a goal as Warrington won 11–3.

The Warrington star was back to his best and, early in the second half against Batley at Wilderspool in January, Calvert, the Batley half-back, was caught in the act of kicking the great man and sent off. Playing against 14 Gallant Youths instead of 15, Warrington coasted to a 20–0 victory.

One Warrington fan, with the initials SWJ, could contain himself no longer and sent a limerick to the *Warrington Examiner*:

There are many team managers fish
But they don't always catch what they wish
Let them try Wilders-pool
And they will, as a rule,
Get a bite from the slippery Fish

As if to prove the point, Fish missed the trip to bottom-of-the-table Keighley with a thumb injury – and Warrington lost 4–0.

Also in January, clubs began adjusting their squads, ready for the start of the Challenge Cup campaign. Warrington signed Welsh forward W Fielding, the captain of Pontynewydd and former team-mate of George Thomas. Fielding was almost 6 feet tall and weighed more than 13 stone, but would only make two appearances for the first team.

Warrington also transferred two reserves, threequarter Ernest Ratcliffe and half-back James Allen, to St Helens to help them get promoted to the First Division. Because the Saints were in the Second Division, Warrington only played them once, at Wilderspool on Easter Monday, and that fixture counted double in the South West Lancashire League, as a home and an away game, and earned four league points. Warrington won 19–3.

Warrington were drawn away to Swinton, another First Division side, in the first round of the Challenge Cup where a crowd of 9,000 witnessed a 0–0 draw. The replay was at Wilderspool the following Wednesday with a 4.30pm kick-off. Many of the town's big works closed at 4pm to allow supporters to get to the match. The 7,000-strong crowd were in for a treat as Warrington won 20–0 with Fish scoring a brilliant try – he shrugged off two attempted tackles to score in the corner – and kicking four goals.

Wigan were the visitors to Wilderspool in the second round, for a tie that attracted a record home crowd of 11,000, generating record receipts of £315. The score at half-time was 0–0 and, after the break, Wigan played for a draw, keeping the ball in the forwards, who outplayed the Warrington pack. Five minutes from time, however, Warrington winger Elliot Harris made a break into the Wigan '25' before being tackled. Warrington's forwards secured the ball from the ensuing scrum and half-backs Robert Bate and Dai Davies handled quickly for centre George Dickenson to dash over for a sensational try. The Wigan players sank to the ground in despair and, although Fish missed the kick at goal by inches, Warrington won 3–0.

Their reward in the third round was a trip to Pontefract and another 11,000 crowd. Pontefract won the toss and played with a strong wind in their favour in the first half. By the break they were leading 4–0 and the home supporters were shouting "Play up Ponty!"

Fish pulled two points back with a penalty from near the half-way line and then kicked another penalty from a difficult angle to tie the scores at 4–4. These, incidentally, were the only penalty goals he kicked all season. Wingers Elliot Harris and Jack Fish then crossed for tries and although Fish was off target with both conversion attempts, Warrington had won 10–4 to reach the semi-finals.

The draw paired Warrington with another Yorkshire side, Bradford, at Broughton where a crowd of 13,000 saw the teams battle out a 3–3 draw, although Bradford were half-a-stone a man heavier.

The replay was at Huddersfield where Warrington took a 3–0 half-time lead thanks to a brilliantly constructed try. Scrum-half Dai Davies collected the ball from a scrum on the Warrington '25' and passed to stand-off Tom Hockenhull. Another pass found centre George Dickenson, who, in turn, found Danny Isherwood, who took the ball at top speed and ran right through the Bradford defence as far as their '25', where he passed to the waiting Jack Fish, who sprinted over.

The excitement was all too much for one Warrington supporter who was stood near the perimeter fence. When Fish received the ball and dashed for the line, the supporter ran on to the pitch and followed the flying winger as fast as his legs would carry him.

"He must have found some speed as he was over the line almost as soon as me," Fish recalled in an interview in 1938. "I heard someone behind me near the line, and dared not look back, being more keen to put the ball down safely for a try. Then I heard a shout of delight, and when I turned I saw this excited spectator wanting to pat me on the back and shake my hand. He was as white as driven snow as the police walked him off. What I said to him I had better not relate!"

After the break, George Dickenson galloped through the Bradford backs to score between the posts, Fish added the goal and Warrington had won 8–0 to reach their second Challenge Cup final.

In the Final, Warrington faced Halifax, the holders, at Salford and, with 17,500 fans there, conceded half-a-stone per man in the forwards.

	Age	Height	Weight
Jack Hallam	25	5ft 8in	11st 6lb
Jack Fish	24	5ft 8in	11st 12lb
Elliot Harris	24	5ft 8in	11st 4lb
Danny Isherwood, capt	27	5ft 9in	10st 12lb
George Dickenson	22	5ft 11in	11st
Dai Davies	24	5ft 9in	10st 6lb
Tom Hockenhull	23	5ft 8in	10st 6lb
George Thomas	22	5ft 9in	13st
Alf Boardman	24	5ft 11in	14st
Dave Morrison	27	5ft 11in	12st 6lb
Arthur Naylor	27	5ft 9in	12st 6lb
Tom Cook	24	5ft 10in	13st
G Jolley	28	5ft 9in	13st 6lb
Elijah Lunt	26	5ft 10in	11st 10lb
Jim Edmondson	23	5ft 10in	12st 4lb

Halifax: W.B. Little, H. Hartley, Joe Riley, W.W. Williams, H. Hawden, A. Nettleton, J. Morley (c), I. Bartle, J.W. Bulmer, G.H. Langhorn, F. Mallinson, Jack Riley, W. Morton, J. Swinbank, R.S. Winskill.
Referee: J.H. Smith (Widnes).

It seemed that every supporter who left Warrington had a 'fish' in his or her coat or hat, workmen having made them by the thousand out of tin, copper, steel or any other suitable material in the local works.

Some supporters, however, were not content with imitation fish. They wanted the real thing and went to Warrington Fish Market on the morning of the match to buy it. Saturday 30 April was a hot, spring day and so the smell among certain sections of the crowd can perhaps better be imagined than described.

Every time Warrington attacked these supporters threw all sorts of fish into the air, to descend like a shower among the spectators. "I never had such an experience after a match," said Fish. "The condition of some of the fish must not have been too good when they obtained it, and when some of the crowd pressed forward after the match to shake hands, well..."

Halifax, with their heavier pack, turned the final into a forward battle and amid allegations of "illegal scrummaging", they won 8–3, although Warrington did have their chances. After 10 minutes, centre George Dickenson had what looked like a perfectly good try disallowed. After 30 minutes, Fish was attempting to field the ball near the Warrington line when it bounced off his knee and over the line for a Halifax scrum. Halifax won the scrum and centre Joe Riley received a pass and rushed over for Hadwen to add an easy goal and make the half-time score 5–0. In the second half, a clever run by Fish set up a try for Dai Davies, who scored in the corner.

Fish missed the kick but, at 5–3, it was anybody's game. Finally, with time running out, Warrington created what looked like a certain try. Danny Isherwood made a break with his winger, Elliot Harris, in support. Isherwood passed at exactly the right time, but the winger stumbled and fell a yard short of the line. This misfortune stunned Warrington and Halifax regained control with a Morley try near the end making the final score 8–3.

Amid all the excitement of the cup run, Jack Fish had also scored the first try in the first international match when England took on Other Nationalities at Wigan's Central Park on the afternoon of Tuesday 5 April. The match had been scheduled to be held at Oldham on New Year's Day, but had been postponed because of frost. Fish, according to reports, made a few "brilliant sweeps", the second of which resulted in a try. The game, dismissed in some quarters as a "sham" international, was a 12-a-side contest and England lost 9–3, but caps were awarded. The teams were as follows:

England: W.B. Little (Halifax), F. Spottiswoode (Oldham), G. Dickenson (Warrington), J. Lomas (Salford), J. Fish (Warrington); J. Baxter (Rochdale Hornets), J. Morley (Halifax), A. Starks (Hull KR, captain), P. Tunney (Salford), J. Riley (Halifax), J.W. Bulmer (Halifax), J. Ferguson (Oldham).

Other Nationalities: D. Smith (Salford), D. Thomas (Salford), T.D. Llewellyn (Leeds), D. Harris (Wigan), D.J. Lewis (Oldham), E. Davies (Wigan), P.J. Brady (Huddersfield), J. Rhapps (Salford), J.G. Moffatt (Leeds), G. Frater (Oldham, captain), D. Thomas (Oldham), H. Buckler (Salford).
Referee: J.H. Smith (Widnes).

Jack Fish in England kit.

Fish, once again, finished as Warrington's leading try scorer and goalkicker, although he had been slightly overshadowed in December when young left winger Tommy Kenyon scored a club record seven of Warrington 'A' team's 11 tries in a 41–0 win over Widnes Rangers.

Warrington reached their third Challenge Cup final in April 1905 and, after the defeats of 1901 and 1904, the Wirepullers finally claimed the trophy, their last as a 15-a-side team.

For five Warrington players in particular it really was a case of third time lucky because captain and full-back Jack Hallam, winger Jack Fish, centres Danny Isherwood and George Dickenson and prop Alf Boardman had all played in both losing finals before finally getting their hands on the cup.

All five – and especially Fish – played major roles in the cup run, as did three forwards signed within a few days of each other in August

33

1904. Welshman Frank Shugars, from Penygraig in the Rhondda Valley, was the first to arrive. Aged 24 and measuring 5 feet 10 inches and 14 stones 6 pounds, he was a specialist scrummager who had been widely tipped to play for Wales during the forthcoming season.

Next came Joe Belton from Birkenhead Wanderers, one of the most accomplished rugby union forwards in Cheshire and a county player. He was 13 stone 10 pounds and 6 feet 2 inches. The Swinton and Lancashire forward Jack Preston completed the trio. A former Swinton captain, Preston had spent five years with the Lions before falling out with the club over training methods. He was 6 feet 1 inch tall and weighed 15 stones.

Preston, unluckily, would miss the final after suffering a knee injury at home to St Helens on Good Friday – eight days before the big match. The injury ruled him out for two reasons. Firstly, and obviously, was the injury itself. Secondly, the injury caused him to miss work and fall foul of the Northern Union bylaw that stated that players had to be at work before they could be considered for selection.

The season got off to an explosive start at Leigh on the first Saturday in September when Warrington won 16–2 despite having two players sent off and losing one more through injury – which reduced them to 12 men at the end. Leigh, with a strong wind at their backs, led 2–0 at half-time before Preston was sent off on his debut – giving them a one-man advantage. Stand-off Dai Davies received his marching orders with the Leigh forward Jack Blackburn. Still, Warrington attacked, even after winger Elliot Harris twisted his knee scoring their fourth try and had to leave the pitch.

Jack Fish, who had been in fine form during the pre-season trial games, scored a try and two goals in the victory but, to the dismay of the committee and the *Warrington Guardian* reporter, he refused to play in the next match, at home to Halifax.

Fish, as the club's best player, thought that he deserved to be paid more money. The committee disagreed. Fish, however, was back in the side for the next match, against Hull at the Boulevard, one of Fish's favourite grounds. Whether Fish or the committee backed down is impossible to say, although Fish was their best player and a winger who the fans would pay good money to watch.

Fish was also a regular in the Lancashire team and, following the game against Yorkshire at Oldham's Watersheddings ground in November, the *Manchester Guardian* was full of praise for his efforts and the way he beat Gomer Gunn, the Bradford and Yorkshire full-back, to score Lancashire's only try: "Every time the ball came along the threequarter line to the man on the extreme left, Fish, a substantial advance was made. He is a fearless fellow this Fish, and well named, for he has all the resource and almost the speed of movement of a hunted trout making for vantage pools in a brook. And he is hard as nails. Snapping up the ball once he shot away with it, but his movement had been anticipated, and a Yorkshire threequarter, already in his stride, bounded after the Warrington man before he had got his stride and brought him down heavily.

"Fish's comrades lifted him up and signalled for the man of sponge and towel. For a minute or two Lancashire people were genuinely anxious. It looked rather worse than a winding. But Fish was soon himself again, and was well enough to kick a goal when the Yorkshire forwards got penalised for a wrong formation in the scrum. Very soon afterwards he smartly intercepted a pass between Yorkshire threequarters, catching it in its flight, but not surely so that it was almost a knock-on, and then bolting for the line. There was only the full back in the way, and Fish went past him easily as if he were merely a dummy figure needing only to be avoided."

Fish was also a marked man. At Leeds in October, he had to leave the pitch with bruised ribs after being singled out for special attention. At St Helens on Boxing Day, he mysteriously received a broken nose.

He also enjoyed duels with other wingers, especially those with big reputations. Against Hull at Wilderspool in January, Fish was up against Arthur Frear, who had won three caps for the Ireland rugby union team before switching codes. The "Warrington crack" – as Fish was often known – outplayed the Irishman throughout and, in the last five minutes, ran past Frear for the third Wirepullers try in a 13–11 win.

At Bradford the following week, Fish used his searing pace to stop a certain try. James 'Jim' Dechan, Bradford's speedy Scottish winger, who was inevitably known as the flying Scotsman, received the ball in space on the half-way line at Park Avenue and raced for the posts. Fish, however, set off in pursuit and dragged him down a foot from the line after a thrilling chase.

Warrington still lost that game 5–3, as they had already lost on their travels at Hull, Leeds, Oldham, Hull KR, Salford and Broughton. They were not going to win the First Division title, but, on their day, they could beat anybody and so fancied their chances in the Challenge Cup.

The Wirepullers were drawn at home to Second Division strugglers Morecambe in the first round and rested some players, but still won 30–0. Vice-captain George Dickenson scored two of their six tries.

Warrington then faced another Second Division team, Keighley, in the second round and luckily escaped with a 3–3 draw after being complacent. The replay, at Keighley the following Tuesday afternoon, drew a crowd of 7,500 with ground record receipts of £255. The Bradford team were there in case they met either side later in the cup.

The game kicked off an hour late – at 5pm – because of the late arrival of the train carrying the Warrington team. Once battle commenced, however, Warrington had little difficulty in winning a poor match 7–0, with prop Alf Boardman scoring their only try. Warrington were later fined 3 guineas (£3, 3 shillings) for their late arrival.

The draw for the third round had already been made and brought Wigan to Wilderspool. The game attracted a then record crowd of 12,750 who paid then record receipts of £406. After 12 minutes, Jack Preston ran in from the half-way line for the first try and added the conversion for a 5–0 lead. Warrington did not look back and a great try from winger Tommy Kenyon put them 8–0 ahead at half-time.

Full-back Jack Hallam followed up and collected his own short kick over the Wigan defence before passing to George Thomas. Thomas, in turn, passed to George Dickenson and the centre sent Kenyon racing over. After the break, Danny Isherwood sent Fish over and the 'irrepressible' added a fine goal to seal a 13–0 victory.

The semi-final was against Bradford at Rochdale where the charges were as follows: 6d ground admission, a further 6d for admission to the enclosure and a further 2s for the stand – making the price of a seat 3s. At the match some Warrington fans, as well as having yellow flowers in their coats, had large cut-out herrings stuck in their caps, in honour of their hero Jack Fish, and they did not have long to wait before the winger scored one of the best tries of his career.

Only five minutes had gone when Fish intercepted a pass on his own 25-yard line and raced clear to meet Gomer Gunn, the Bradford full-back. Fish produced one or two subtle feints at half-way, while still at full speed, to leave the Bradford man flat-footed and score between the posts. "As I went towards him my body began to sway as I prepared for my swerve," Fish recalled in an interview in 1936. "Gunn swayed with me this way and that until in the end he beat himself. He told me afterwards that I had mesmerised him and that he had fallen off his balance in trying to sway into the tackle that would get me."

Jack Preston added the goal and although Bradford had the heavier and stronger pack, they never recovered. Preston added a second goal and, in front of a crowd of 15,000, Warrington won 7–2.

For the final against Hull KR, 12 special trains left Arpley Station for Leeds, taking more than 5,000 Warrington fans to Headingley. The team lined up as follows; Bill Harmer replaced the injured Jack Preston:

Jack Hallam (full-back)	26	5ft 8in	11st 6lb
Jack Fish (left wing)	25	5ft 8in	11st 12lb
Danny Isherwood (left centre)	28	5ft 8in	10st 12lb
George Dickenson (right centre)	23	5ft 10in	11st
Tommy Kenyon (right wing)	21	5ft 7in	10st 6lb
Dai Davies (half-back)	25	5ft 8in	10st 6lb
Ernie Brookes (half-back)	21	5ft 7in	11st 8lb

George Thomas (forward)	23	5ft 8in	12st
Alf Boardman (forward)	25	5ft 10in	14st 12lb
Arthur Naylor (forward)	28	5ft 9in	12st 6lb
G Jolley (forward)	29	5ft 9in	13st 8lb
Frank Shugars (forward)	25	5ft 11in	14st 9lb
Joe Belton (forward)	26	6ft 2in	13st 10lb
Walter Swift (forward)	25	5ft 11in	12st 2lb
Bill Harmer (forward)	22	5ft 11in	12st 2lb

Hull KR: H. Sinclair, W. Madley, A.W. Robinson, W. Phipps, G.H. West, J. Barry, J. Gordon; A. Starks, A. Kemp, W.T. Osborne, A. Spackman, A. Windle, G. Ellis, F. Gorman, D. Reed.
Referee: J. Bruckshaw (Stockport).

There was no score at half-time, but two second-half tries from the one and only Jack Fish gave Warrington a 6–0 victory and the Challenge Cup for the first time in front of a crowd of 19,438.

His first try came five minutes after the interval from a scrum under the Hull KR posts. Warrington won quick ball and Dai Davies broke away and passed to Danny Isherwood. The centre passed to Fish who shrugged off two tacklers to ground the ball in the corner. Fish, proving he was only human after all, missed the kick.

The second try followed a break by Ernie Brookes, with Fish in support. On reaching the Hull KR full-back, Brookes simply passed to Fish, the winger's pace did the rest and he touched down by the posts. Captain Jack Hallam took the conversion but hit the post.

Hallam received the cup from the wife of Mr F. Lister, the Northern Union president, amid much cheering. The team arrived back at Arpley Station at 9pm and were greeted by a large crowd of supporters – and the Borough Brass Band. A tour of the town followed and ended at the Town Hall, shortly before 11pm. Finally, after speeches, the team went to their headquarters, the Roebuck pub on Bridge Street, for more celebrations. The band played *Poor cock robin* – in honour of Hull KR.

The following Saturday the team were entertained to dinner at the Lion Hotel. There was also a civic reception at the Town Hall and a tour of the town, with the cup, in an illuminated tram. At the front of the tram the letters 'WFC' shone out, with '1905' highlighted at the back. Crowds in Horsemarket Street held sticks aloft which had tin fish fixed in a slot at the top, another tribute to Warrington's best player.

The team were also invited to dinner at Walton Hall, home of the wealthy Greenall family, on 23 May. A special menu was printed, which featured a fish with a primrose and blue ribbon in its mouth, and listed such treats as Dee salmon, fricassee of chicken, roast beef, roast lamb, peas, new potatoes and strawberry and lemon dessert. To complete the formal celebrations, there was a concert at the Parr Hall.

37

The 1905 Challenge Cup winning team: Back: I. Hackett (trainer), W. Harmer, F. Shugars, J. Preston, A.E. Boardman, J. Belton, G. Jolley, F. Heesom (trainer); middle: W. Swift, T. Kenyon, G. Dickenson, J. Hallam (capt), D. Isherwood, J. Fish, T. Cook; kneeling: G. Thomas, D.A. Davies, E. Brookes, A. Naylor.

Jack Fish with the Challenge Cup.

A newspaper cartoon of Warrington's 1905 Challenge Cup triumph.

The menu from the end of season dinner in 1904-05.

5. Lifting the Cup as captain

"He showed the old touch of genius, and scored a try that perhaps no other man on the field could have made possible."

Jack Fish scored the most profitable try of his career against Wigan at Central Park on Saturday 18 February 1905 – although he did not know it at the time. He crossed the try line in the corner and started heading for the posts to make the conversion attempt easier. On seeing this, Peter 'Bucky' Green, the Wigan speedster, sprinted across the field in an unsuccessful attempt to head him off.

Wigan supporters were astonished at his raw pace and suggested that he was a faster man than Fish. Warrington fans were having none of that and so the arguments continued. Eventually, it was agreed that the two men would meet in a winner-takes-all sprint race over 80 yards at Springfield Park in Wigan on Saturday 23 September to settle the matter once-and-for-all. The prize was £100, about £10,000 in today's money.

This was a substantial sum of money and so Fish put in some serious training. He gave up work for a month and went into camp under the watchful eye of Jim Heesom, a local sprint coach and former Warrington forward. They were based at the Longford Hotel in Warrington and looked after by the licensee, Joe Horlock.

It was a strict regime, worthy of a champion boxer: early to bed, early to rise; specially-prepared food; long walks and, of course, plenty of sprint work. Come the big day, Fish said he felt "in the pink of condition" – 'Bucky' Green never stood a chance.

Green won the toss and picked the lane nearest to his 1,000 supporters, but, when the starter gave the signal, Fish made a fantastic start and had put daylight between the two after only 10 yards. Fish increased his advantage with every stride and was able to glance at his opponent at half-way. He eventually won by four yards.

Years later Fish recalled: "I was off my mark like the shot of a gun, and I am not boasting when I say I had the match won after 30 yards. At half-way, there was not the slightest danger; indeed I could afford to ease up and I won with the greatest of ease by three or four yards. 'Bucky' Green came to me after the match, shook hands with me and said he did not think I was so fast."

Fish was delighted and so were the dozens of Warrington supporters who had backed him to win. Fish was now 26 and at the height of his powers, but, two weeks later, he suffered a broken shoulder bone in the act of scoring Lancashire's only try in a 3–3 draw against Cumberland at Wigan's Central Park. Fish touched down in the corner, after Salford's James Lomas had created an opening, and then had to be helped from the pitch.

Fish's injury meant that he missed out on a small piece of club history on Saturday, 28 October 1905 when the Warrington players wore numbers on their jerseys for the first time for the visit of Leigh in the second round of the Lancashire Cup. Without Fish, Warrington lost 5–2 to a Leigh team who were not wearing numbers.

He was out of action for two months, but not out of the news. Early in December, for example, while still recovering from his broken shoulder, he refereed a friendly match between Warrington Tramways and Salford Tramways at Victoria Park, which Warrington won 6–5 and which was followed by a "substantial" dinner at the Lion Hotel.

Fish returned to the Warrington team at Dewsbury on 16 December and confirmed his return to fitness by playing six games in the next two weeks. The England selectors, therefore, had no hesitation in naming him in the side to face Other Nationalities on New Year's Day 1906. Again, the match was at Central Park and the teams lined up as follows:

England: T. Barton (St Helens), J. Leytham (Wigan), W.J. Eagers (Hunslet), J. Lomas (Salford), J. Fish (Warrington), T. Surman (Bradford), T. Hockenhull (Warrington), F. Webster (Leeds), W. Brooke (Hunslet), H. Wilson (Hunslet), I. Bartle (Halifax), J. Cole (Castleford), A. Smith (Oldham), R. Silcock (Leigh), F. Lee (St Helens).
Other Nationalities: G. Gunn (Bradford); W. Jowett (Hull KR), W. Jones (Wigan), T. Llewellyn (Leeds), A. Hogg (Broughton Rangers), S. James (Broughton Rangers), W. James (Broughton Rangers), D. Rees (Salford), F. Watkins (Wigan), F. Shugars (Warrington), H. Francis (Bradford), A.W. Little (Wigan), G. Thomas (Warrington), D. Davies (Swinton), W.T. Osborne (Hull KR).
Referee: F Renton (Hunslet).

The match ended in a 3–3 draw with Salford's James Lomas scoring a try for England and Willie James of Broughton Rangers doing likewise for Other Nationalities in front of a respectable crowd of 8,000. That, however, was of little importance to Warrington supporters because Jack Fish had again been injured.

At first, it was thought that he had suffered a severe sprain to his left ankle, but when he was still in pain three weeks later the club sent him to see a specialist in Manchester. The specialist discovered that Fish had sustained a broken tibia and so his leg was encased in plaster. Fish was out of action for a further two months.

Away from rugby league, the parliamentary constituency of Warrington was part of the Liberal Landslide at the 1906 General Election, which was held from 12 January to 8 February and at which neither Jack Fish (being working class) nor his wife, Fanny, (being a woman) were allowed to vote. The sitting Conservative MP, Robert Pierpoint, lost his seat to the Liberal Arthur Henry Crosfield, aged 40, the son of Joseph Crosfield, the soap manufacturer.

Arthur Crosfield was re-elected in January 1910, but then lost the seat back to the Conservatives and their candidate Harold Smith 11 months later. The following year, 1911, Crosfield cut many of his links with Warrington by selling the Joseph Crosfield and sons company.

With the proceeds of that sale, Crosfield built a Georgian-style mansion in Highgate, north London, named Witanhurst, and said to be the largest house in the capital outside Buckingham Palace. Designed by architect George Hubbard, and built between 1913 and 1920 on a five acre estate, Witanhurst boasted 65 rooms spread across three floors and including 25 bedrooms.

The ballroom was 70 feet long and 20 feet high and had oak flooring and timber wall panels in walnut, with carved cornices embellished with gold leaf. In July 2008, it was reported that Yelena Baturina, the wife of the former Mayor of Moscow and a billionaire in her own right, had bought the property for an estimated £50million and was to spend £40million restoring it to its former glory.

After selling Joseph Crosfield and sons, Crosfield remained a director of the company that owned the *Warrington Examiner* newspaper and, in 1915, was knighted in recognition of his public services.

Sir Arthur died on 22 September, 1938, aged 73, while travelling by express train with his wife and valet to Cannes. The train had just passed through Le Muy when Sir Arthur opened the door of his sleeping compartment and made his way along the corridor. He apparently mistook an exit for another door and fell from the train.

Fish missed 25 of Warrington's 41 matches during the 1905–06 season and, to add insult to injury of course, neither of the two serious injuries he suffered at Central Park was sustained while playing for the Wirepullers.

Without Fish, Warrington lost in the first round of the Challenge Cup at Batley and could only finish 15th out of the 31 teams in the Northern Rugby League. The critics who said that Warrington were a "one-man team" could feel vindicated.

To further prove their point, Fish returned to action for the last seven games of the season, helping the team to achieve five wins and a draw – their best run of the entire campaign. The Fish factor also had a damaging effect on the club's finances. At the annual general meeting at the Co-operative Hall in Cairo Street in May 1906 it was announced that the club had lost £300 – about £30,000 in today's money – that season.

By returning for the end of the season Fish played in Warrington's last match as a 15-a-side team. He scored a try and kicked two goals in a 15–2 victory over Hunslet at Wilderspool on 28 April. At the start of the following season he also played in Warrington's first match as a 13-a-side team, and kicked a goal in an 8–8 draw at Leigh on 1 September.

Over the summer of 1906, the Northern Union decided to abolish the flank forwards to make play more exciting – and reduce club's wage bills. It was cheaper to pay 13 players than 15. In another sign of growing confidence as a sport in its own right, the Northern Union had already scrapped its working clause and professional committee, making life much easier for club secretaries.

Fish, newly-appointed as Warrington captain for the 1906–07 season, revelled in the extra space created on the pitch by having four fewer players and scored a club record 30 points in the 50–3 thrashing of Huddersfield at Wilderspool in October, beating the 29 points he had scored against Goole in the Challenge Cup in 1900. Fish's haul was made up of four tries and nine goals and he completed the rout by racing in from half-way for a sensational try.

Victories over Leigh, Barrow and Oldham – all at Wilderspool – earned Warrington a place in the Lancashire Cup final against Broughton Rangers at Central Park on Saturday, 1 December. A crowd of 14,048 – including many neutrals and 3,500 from Warrington – turned out to watch the game, but were left deflated by an injury in the sixth minute.

Jack Fish, again, suffered a broken right forearm in a tackle – two bones were broken – and had to leave the field, reducing his team to 12 men for the rest of the match. It was Fish's third serious injury at his 'bogey ground' in the space of 14 months. George Thomas was pulled out of the pack to take Fish's place on the wing.

After treatment, Fish returned to watch the rest of the match with his right arm in a splint. Despite being a man short Warrington only trailed 5–0 at half-time but were 13–0 down before George Dickenson scored a try from Thomas' inside pass. To further sum up Warrington's afternoon, vice-captain Jack Preston's conversion attempt hit the post.

Broughton then stretched their lead to 15–3 with a penalty before Ernie Brookes scored a second Warrington try to make the final score 15–6 and leave everyone present wondering what might have been.

To help replace the injured Fish, the Warrington committee signed one of Widnes's best players, James H. 'Jimmy' Tilley, for an undisclosed fee in December. He could play at full-back or anywhere in the threequarters and would prove to be a very useful addition to the team. Over the next six years he would make 162 appearances and the courage he displayed on the field would help him to win the Distinguished Conduct Medal for "conspicuous gallantry" during the First World War.

Fish's comeback game was against Liverpool City at Wilderspool on 18 February and he marked his return with a hat-trick of tries. He did not, however, take on the goalkicking duties. That was left to Tom Hockenhull and Jack Preston and between them they missed 14 of the 16 conversions, so that Warrington only won 52–0. If every kick had been successful, the score would have been a club record 80 points.

Defeats at Swinton and Halifax in March meant that Warrington could no longer qualify for the newly-introduced top four play-offs, but allowed them to concentrate fully on the Challenge Cup. Warrington were drawn at home to Batley, one of their bogey teams, in the first round, but beat the Gallant Youths for the first time in the competition – after three previous defeats.

Hull visited Wilderspool in round two when four goals from Fish helped Warrington to a 16–0 victory. A trip to Huddersfield in the quarter-finals attracted an attendance of 14,000 – one of the biggest gates in Yorkshire that season – and again Fish was to the fore with a try and two goals in a 15–7 win.

Optimism was in the air, although down the road at Widnes the Chemicals were facing closure and so, in April, Warrington sent them £20, equivalent to about £2,000 in today's money, to help them survive.

In the build-up to the semi-final against Swinton at Central Park, Warrington enjoyed a week of quiet preparation, including brine baths, although Fish, their prized asset, was given some specialist sprint training. Swinton were swept aside 21–0 in front of 12,000 fans, in Warrington's easiest match of the competition, with Fish contributing two tries and two goals so that he had scored in every round.

The final was against Oldham at Wheater's Field, Broughton, on Saturday 27 April and was Warrington's last match of the season. A crowd of 18,000 – including 6,000 Warrington supporters and many neutrals – turned out to watch the action. The teams lined up as follows:

Warrington: J. Tilley; J. Fish (c), D. Isherwood, I. Taylor, E. Brookes, T. Hockenhull, S. Lees, G. Heath, A. Boardman, G. Thomas, F. Shugars, J. Belton, A. Naylor.
Oldham: R.L. Thomas, T. White, S.H. Irvin, W. Dixon, G. Tyson, A. Lees (c), M. Yewlett, J. Ferguson, H. Topham, A. Smith, J. Vowles, A. Avery, J.H. Wilkinson.
Referee: F. Renton (Hunslet).

Bert Avery, the veteran Oldham forward, scored the game's first try despite a strong tackle by centre Danny Isherwood, before a Fish penalty goal made the score 3–2. Just before half-time Warrington's George Heath touched down an Ernie Brookes grubber kick but referee Frank Renton ruled that the veteran forward was offside and disallowed the score. At half-time, Warrington tweaked their back division, as they had done at Huddersfield in the quarter-final, and switched winger Ernie Brookes with stand-off Tom Hockenhull to make better use of Brookes's pace.

In one frantic attack near the Oldham line, Warrington prop Frank Shugars and centre Ike Taylor clashed heads, which meant that both had to go off the pitch for treatment, reducing the Wirepullers to 11 men. Still, Warrington attacked and although Fish appeared to be tackled close to the line he managed to get a pass away to scrum-half Sammy Lees who dodged a couple of defenders and touched down.

It was a magical moment for the Oldham-born player who had been discarded by his hometown club because they did not think he was big enough. Fish added the goal to make the score 7–3 just before Shugars and Taylor returned with bandaged heads.

Fish now took matters into his own hands. He dribbled a loose ball past his opposite number, caught it on the bounce, swerved past the full-back and sprinted to the line for a sensational try. One Warrington supporter in the crowd, who was a cornet player, sounded the *Last Post* on Oldham's hopes just before Fish added the goal.

Hockenhull added a third try near the end, which Fish again converted to make the final score 17–3. After Fish received the cup from Mrs Cooke, the wife of the president of the Northern Union, he made a short speech, and players and officials from both clubs were treated to dinner at the Grosvenor Hotel in Manchester by the Union.

The Warrington team arrived back at Central Station at 8.30pm to be greeted by a huge crowd. The Borough Brass Band played *See the conquering hero comes* and then boarded the first of two buses, with the team and the cup on the second.

Both buses then toured the town while fans cheered and let off fireworks. The team arrived at the Town Hall – only to find it closed – and then continued their parade to a party at the Bridge Inn. The following Tuesday evening, the team toured the town in an illuminated tram, lit by 850 light bulbs, to again show off the trophy. Union Jacks were displayed at each end of the tram and the years 1905 and 1907 picked out in coloured lights.

The players could also bask in the glory of the many favourable match reports, especially the 28-year-old Fish. 'Philistine' in the Manchester-based *Athletic News* wrote: "Warrington played a strong game, and played it with a will from start to finish. Tilley proved his value in the first few minutes, and his splendid services had no little influence on the team, especially the forwards.

"Fish's try compensated for everything he had done or not done during the other parts of the match. He gave one the impression that he had lost some of his speed and a little of his pluck until that brilliant effort and magnificent piece of opportunism put a gilt-edged halo on his head, and restored him to the pinnacle of fame."

'Flaneur' in the *Leeds Mercury* wrote: "I have no doubt that nearly everyone had been saying 'This is not the Fish of old' throughout the game, for the famous left wing had shown a great want of thought in his dropping out, and had been playing in a very lackadaisical fashion.

"There had been, indeed, nothing to distinguish him from the very mediocre club three-quarter, and one had come to the conclusion that Fish had had his day, when his great chance came. Perhaps he had been waiting for some big opportunity. When it came he showed the old touch of genius, and scored a try that perhaps no other man on the field could have made possible."

There are, of course, two sides to every story and Oldham supporters maintained that Fish's pass to Sammy Lees for the first Warrington try had been forward and that the winger had pushed his opposite number out of the way before scoring his sensational solo try.

The *Oldham Evening Chronicle* said: "All the luck was with Oldham's opponents. Everything they did came right, and Oldham could do nothing right, whilst they were unfortunate in the matter of incurring penalties. I have not the remotest intention of questioning Mr Renton's bona fides, but he certainly was extremely severe on Oldham for trivial offences, and in the case of the offside rule he frequently penalised Oldham, where their side had given the Warrington player fully the required distance before playing, whilst on the other hand he noticeably neglected to penalise the Wirepullers for the same offence and others.

"On one occasion, certainly, he did order the ball back when Heath seemed to have scored for Warrington, but frequently he allowed them to profit by breaches of the rules. Two of their tries were gained under these circumstances. Sam Lees received the ball from a forward pass when he scored, and when Fish scored his sensational try he ought to have been stopped before he had gone a yard. He and Tyson were both going for the ball together, Tyson being in front of him, and, seeing that the Oldham man was certain to get it, Fish deliberately charged him in the back and flung him, although he had not the ball in his possession."

The *Oldham Standard* said: "After Oldham having had so much the best of the game, it almost appears incredible that they should be beaten by such a score. The score, however, by no means represents the game. Warrington were the luckiest team in the world to escape a score against them when Fish scored for them. Fortune appeared to have deserted Oldham with a vengeance, and whatever luck there was knocking about fell Warrington's way. Apart from that, the game was worth going miles to see despite the adverse criticism of a certain Manchester contemporary. I was not very greatly impressed with the Oldham attack; in fact, that was just where the team was let down."

The *Manchester Guardian* commented: "The turbulent noisiness of Deansgate compared with the pandemonium at the crowded football ground was as the murmur of a summer sea to the roar of rock-torn surges in a tempest. Every tenth Warrington man seemed to possess a rattle, and lifting arms as well as voices they made the most ear-wracking din that was ever raised by high-spirited football enthusiasts packed together in a lump.

"From the moment the players appeared until the match was over there was a continuous raging of strange sounds, and when the Warrington side secured their commanding advantage towards the end of the game the crash of the tumult reached a frenzied crescendo that seemed to impel individual men to do strangely eccentric things, as, for example, to smash umbrellas and walking sticks on the roof of the stands with a deliberate spirit of destructiveness which meant only that human speech and human voice failed to express sufficiently the delirious delight of the moment.

"Many during the football season that is gone have uttered jeremiads on the Northern Union game; they have spoken of it as a thing with its fortunes in the grave, and so on. But Saturday showed that it is yet a game that can bring together 20,000 people and give them cause for great demonstrations of high spirits and good humour, even on a cold and drizzling afternoon."

The *Yorkshire Post* said: "While the match had its fine individual performances, as here described, it is quite impossible for any rugby man of knowledge, and experience to pretend to be enthusiastic over the class of football which the game produced. In the first half one seemed to be viewing one of the worst features of the handling code – that of fierce and indiscriminate rushing and charging – without its compensations in skilful handling and quick combined running. There was an improvement in the second half, when the ardour of some of the men had partly played itself out, but even then there was far too much punting and 'marking' and wild rushing, and but for the great efforts of Fish and Hockenhull the match would have had to be spoken of as having little else but rush and excitement to recommend it."

Fred Cooper, the former Bradford threequarter, writing in the *Daily Mail*, added: "Fish, who, in my opinion, played one of the worst games of his career, contributed one dribble which will live long in the memory of those who saw it. At the same time Fish was decidedly lucky in being allowed to go on with his dribble which culminated in a try, for he deliberately pushed with his hands an opponent to whom the ball was going, and his side should have been penalised. I think they (Oldham) would have won if the referee had noticed Fish's action in preventing his opponent getting to the ball. Up to that point Oldham had had the best of the game; afterwards they were decidedly the inferior side, and at the end were well beaten."

The *Manchester Courier* said: "The Watersheddings team did the most pressing for half-way through the second half, but then it was seen that Warrington were in possession of that reserve strength necessary in such a strenuous struggle. Cup-tie games are not, as a rule, good expositions of football, but this was one of the best of its kind. Our Yorkshire friends considered it a poor game, but what else could one expect from them when only Lancashire clubs were engaged."

The *Liverpool Courier* outlined: "One must acknowledge that Warrington were the fitter set, and too much praise cannot be bestowed on the committee in having their men so fit for such an important contest. The big, lusty forwards were especially nippy, and they were seen to great advantage in the closing stages. The superiority of the Wirepullers was demonstrated to the full, and the confidence of the backs was in direct contrast to that of the opposition."

The following Saturday the Warrington players received their gold winners' medals at a dinner at the Lion Hotel and were asked to say a few words, although a rather reluctant Jimmy Tilley said he would rather face 13 players on the pitch than make a speech.

Little did anyone realise that it would be 43 years – and two World Wars – before the club would win the cup again. For one Warrington forward, however, the glory of the cup run would soon fade into insignificance.

Prop Alf Boardman, a general labourer, returned home to 4 Oldham Street for dinner on Monday, 13 May – just 16 days after the final – to be told by his wife Nellie that their three-year-old son Thomas had been drowned in a clay pit at Latchford. The child's dead body was in the house.

The clay pit was on private land, but the area was regularly used as a playground by local children. At an inquest two days later, a jury returned a verdict of accidental death, but said that the landowners, the Warrington Brick and Tile Company, had a moral obligation to fill in the pit as soon as possible. The Coroner said that the people who lived in Oldham Street had no gardens and no servants to look after their children. The children had to play in the street and elsewhere. The loss of his son had a profound effect on Boardman and he, too, died before his time, aged just 37, on 12 November 1918.

Warrington stalwart Mr J.E. (Ted) Warren, meanwhile, was toasting the lucky number seven. In 1877, he joined the Padgate club. In 1887, he was Warrington captain. In 1897, he was elected president of the Northern Union. Finally, in 1907, he was Warrington's president when the Wirepullers won the cup.

After Warrington won the Challenge Cup in 1905, the club had the words "Warrington" "1904/5" and "J Hallam" engraved on the silver disc on the trophy's plinth to record the season of the success and the name of the captain.

After the victory in 1907, for some unknown reason, the name of the captain – J Fish – was omitted. This mistake only came to light – and was corrected – after Warrington won the Challenge Cup again in 1950, 43 years later.

Since then, Jack Hallam and Jack Fish have been joined on the plinth by "H. Bath 1949–50", "joint capts A. Naughton E. Frodsham 1953–4", "A. Murphy 1973–4", "A. Morley 2008–9" and "A. Morley 2009–10".

At the start of the 1907–08 season, Fish was again selected for the Lancashire county trial match, which, on this occasion, was played at Wilderspool on Monday 30 September. On this occasion, however, for the first time, Fish was not picked in the "Probables" line-up, he was relegated to the "Possibles" and was selected alongside Danny Isherwood, his regular centre at Warrington.

Fish, who was three months short of his 30th birthday, made the selectors pay for their snub by scoring two tries to help the Possibles achieve a shock 17–11 victory against the supposedly stronger side.

The selectors soon realised the error of their ways and named Fish in their side for the opening game of the County Championship against Cumberland at Wheater's Field, Broughton on Saturday 5 October.

Again, Fish did not let them down, and scored Lancashire's only try in a 7–3 defeat in what was to be his last appearance for the red rose county. The try was Fish's 16th in 16 county appearances.

Cartoon of Warrington's triumph in the 1907 Challenge Cup Final.

A souvenir of when Jack Fish captained Warrington to win
the Challenge Cup for the second time in three years.

6. Jack Fish versus Dally Messenger

"The result was a badly-wounded Fish who gave a mighty grunt and was violently sick."

Every rugby league supporter in Australia has heard of Dally Messenger because every year the Dally M Medal is awarded to the country's best and fairest player. The honour was instigated in 1980 as a lasting tribute to Australia's first great rugby league star and is usually presented by the Australian Prime Minister at the Dally M Awards Night. The Dally M, then, is Australia's "Man of Steel" award.

The man himself, Herbert Henry Messenger, was born in Balmain, New South Wales on 12 April 1883 – making him five years younger than Jack Fish – and won two caps for the Australian rugby union team, the Wallabies, as a threequarter before switching codes in 1907. Like Fish, he had a stocky build – he was 5 feet 8 inches tall and weighed 12 stones 6 pounds – and was a mesmerising runner.

Messenger made two rugby league tours of England: in 1907–08 with New Zealand, who were dubbed the All Golds by the rugby union-loving press, and in 1908–09 with Australia's first touring team, the Kangaroos. During the second tour he was offered contracts by Manchester United and Tottenham Hotspur, but refused them on the grounds that association football was decadent.

Messenger faced Fish and Warrington on two occasions. Warrington won one match and drew the other with both men taking the individual honours for their teams by playing outstandingly well and scoring tries. Warrington were so impressed with Messenger that they tried to sign him during the summer of 1909, but more of that later.

The All Golds' tour was a huge success and their visit to Warrington on Saturday 21 December, 1907 was regarded as a red letter day in the history of the club. The touring party arrived in Warrington by train on the morning of the match and was treated to a civic reception at the Town Hall and a light lunch at the Lion Hotel on Bridge Street, where they stayed for two nights. They were introduced to Sir Gilbert Greenall, of the famous brewing family, and Mr Arthur H. Crosfield, the Liberal MP for Warrington.

Heavy rain on the morning of the match dashed hopes of Wilderspool hosting a record crowd, but 8,000 supporters still turned out to see the All Golds in action and there were even ringside seats for club members.

Before kick-off, they performed their war chant, now universally known as the Haka, with captain 'Bumper' Wright taking the lead. The words had already been printed in the local press:

Ka mate; ka mate; ka ora; ka ora;
Ka mate; ka mate; ka ora; ka ora;
Tenei te tangata; Puhuru huru;
Nana e pike mai. Whaka whiti t era.
Hupanei, Hupanei, Hupanei, Hupanei; Whiti t era

Translation:
There is going to be a fight between us,
May it mean death to you and life to us.
We will fight on until one side is vanquished;
So long as the daylight lasts we are here to continue battle,
To be killed or to be victorious.

Warrington included 10 of the team who had won the Challenge Cup eight months earlier. The changes were George Dickenson, Jack Jenkins and Bill Harmer. Dickenson took over from Danny Isherwood as Fish's centre, Jack Jenkins replaced Tom Hockenhull at scrum-half and Bill Harmer replaced George Heath in the pack. The teams lined up as follows:
Warrington: J.H. Tilley, J. Fish, G. Dickenson, I. Taylor, E. Brookes, S. Lees, J. Jenkins, G. Thomas, W. Harmer, F. Shugars, J. Belton, A. Naylor, A. Boardman.
New Zealand: H.S. Turtill (Christchurch), H.H. Messenger (Eastern Suburbs), H.F. Rowe (Auckland), E. Wrigley (Wairarapa), W.T. Tyler (Auckland), L.B. Todd (Auckland), R.J. Wynyard (Auckland), H.R. Wright (captain, Wellington), W.M. Trevarthen (Auckland), C.J. Pearce (Christchurch), D. Gilchrist (Wellington), T.W. Cross (Wellington), C.A. Byrne (Wellington).
Referee: J.M. Lumley (Leeds).

Jack Fish was the first of the two superstars to strike, and scored in the corner to put Warrington ahead. Although George Thomas missed the kick at goal he soon added a penalty to put Warrington 5–0 in front. Messenger responded by reducing the arrears with a mighty penalty goal, kicked from the half-way line and from a difficult angle.

Messenger then dashed in near the corner before he touched down at the posts and kicked the conversion to put New Zealand 7–5 ahead at half-time. In the second half, Warrington's luck seemed to be out when Thomas dribbled the ball over the line, but saw it run dead before he could touch down. Then, finally, captain Sammy Lees passed to Ike Taylor and the centre crossed for the match-winning try and an 8–7 victory.

The match was followed by high tea at the Lion, where the players from both sides were presented with souvenir cigarette cases, and a trip to the Warrington Hippodrome to see the pantomime *Aladdin*. The following day, the tourists visited Knutsford and had tea at the Royal

George Hotel. On the Monday they were given a tour of the Crosfield's works at Bank Quay before leaving town with some golden memories.

The First Kangaroos visited Wilderspool for the first time on Saturday 22 November 1908 when, for the first time, match programmes were on sale, priced 1d.

These were, in fact, match cards – made of card rather than paper – and folded in half. They were issued for each game throughout the tour with the proceeds going to the tourists, to help fund their costs. Team line-ups were deliberately withheld from the newspapers before the games in an attempt to boost sales.

The Australians, like the All Golds, performed a pre-match war cry, which was included in the match card, together with its translation.

Wallee Mullara, Choomooroo ting-al,
Nah! Nah! Nah! Nah!
Canai, Barrang, Warrang, Warrang,
Yallah, Yallah, Yallah, Yallah,
Ah; Jaleeba booga boorooloong,
Yarnah meei; meei, meei,
Neeyarra, Weyarra, Jaleeba, Cahwoon,
Cooeewah, Cooeewah, warr, wooh

Translation
We are a race of fighters, descended from the war gods,
Beware! Beware! Beware! Beware!
Where we fight there will be great bloodshed,
Go! Go! Go! Go!
We are powerful but, merciful, are you friends? Good, good,
The Kangaroo is dangerous when at bay;
Come on, come on, to death

Surprisingly, perhaps, the visit of the Australians attracted a crowd of just 5,000 to Wilderspool – down 3,000 on the gate for the game against the All Golds the previous year. Part of the reason for this was that the admission charge for the popular side of the ground had been increased to one shilling, much to the annoyance of some supporters. Australia were also without their best player, Messenger, who was injured.

Warrington included Lewis Treharne, a speedy winger of Cornish extraction who had been signed from Wigan the previous month, and brothers Alf and Peter Boardman in the pack. Warrington were numbered from one to 13, while the Australians wore squad numbers, the first time that had happened for a match at Wilderspool.

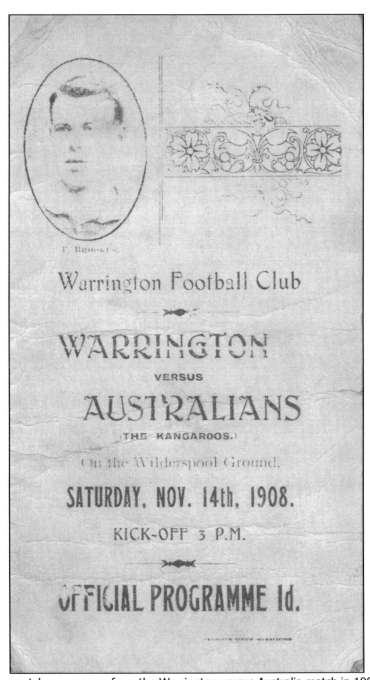

The match programme from the Warrington versus Australia match in 1908.

Warrington: **1** J.H. Tilley, **2** J. Fish, **3** G. Dickenson, **4** I. Taylor, **5** L. Treharne,
6 E. Brookes, **7** J. Jenkins, **8** A. Boardman, **9** P. Boardman, **10** G. Thomas,
11 W O'Neill, **12** W.H. Dowell, **13** J.W. Chesters.
Australia: **2** M. Bolewski, **12** W. Bailey, **14** A. Morton **21** J. Devereaux,
5 D. Frawley, **10** S. Deane, **8** A Holloway, **32** L. O'Malley, **16** J. Abercrombie,
17 A. Burdon, **24** R. Graves, **20** J. Davis, **35** P. Walsh.

Before the match, Dan Frawley, the Australian winger who would have
to face Fish, asked the more experienced Bill Hardcastle for advice.
"Bung right into his Darby Kelly," was the reply, with 'Darby Kelly' being
the Australian rhyming slang for belly.

The Rugby League News, published in Australia in July 1922, takes
up the story. "Dan did as he was told, and the result was a badly-
wounded Fish, for as the Aussie crashed into his midriff he gave a
mighty grunt, and was violently sick. It was some time before he
recovered but he had a great respect for Daniel from that day on."

Soon afterwards, Fish had an opportunity to put Warrington ahead
with a penalty, but his attempt hit the post. The winger more than
made up for that, however, when he shook off Frawley to touch down
for the game's opening try after good play by Welsh forward Billy
O'Neill and captain George Dickenson. Ernie Brookes missed the kick
and so the half-time score was 3–0.

After the break, centre Ike Taylor scored the second Warrington try.
He took a pass from Brookes and made a bee line to the posts. Fish
added the goal to put Warrington 8–0 in front. Australia pulled a try
back, but on the stroke of full-time Dickenson kicked a drop-goal – the
ball dropped on to the crossbar and bounced over – to make the final
score 10–3.

One of the many highlights of the game had been the duel between
the two full-backs. Australia's Mick Bolewski (nicknamed 'Bottle of
Whisky' by English crowds) showed the greater pace, but Warrington's
Jimmy Tilley was better at kicking and fielding kicks. After the match,
both teams had dinner at the Lion Hotel on Bridge Street. The
Kangaroos were clearly not happy about losing and challenged
Warrington to another match near the end of their epic 46-match trip.

This game was held on Saturday 13 February 1909 – a beautiful
spring day – and Messenger was back to renew his rivalry with Jack
Fish. Both men played on the wing and, because the ground admission
price had been slashed from 1s to 6d, were cheered on by a better-
than-expected 7,000 crowd. The gate receipts were £150, of which the
tourists received 60 per cent.

To add to the international flavour, Warrington included five players
who had been signed from Welsh rugby union in scrum-half Jack
Jenkins (Llwynpia) and forwards Billy Dowell (Pontypool), Billy O'Neill

(Cardiff), George Thomas (Newport) and Frank Shugars (Penygraig). The teams lined up as follows:

Warrington: J.H. Tilley, J. Fish, G. Dickenson, I. Taylor, L. Treharne, E. Brookes, J. Jenkins; W.H. Dowell, W. O'Neill, G. Thomas, A. Boardman, J. Belton, F. Shugars.

Australia: C. Hedley (Glebe); H.H. Messenger (Easts), D. Frawley (Easts), W.G. Heidke (Bundaberg, Queensland), T.A. Anderson (Souths), A. Butler (Souths), A. Holloway (Glebe); R.H. Graves (Balmain), T.J. McCabe (Glebe), L. O'Malley (Easts), P. Walsh (Newcastle), A.S. Hennessey (Souths), W.A. Cann (Souths).

Referee: H. Farrar (Keighley).

Messenger kicked off; the Kangaroos were soon on the attack and soon in front, with Messenger kicking a penalty goal from near half-way. Warrington retaliated and George Thomas was held up inches from the line. The pressure was maintained and Arthur Holloway, the Australian scrum-half, lost the ball for Jack Jenkins, the Warrington scrum-half, to pick up and score. Fish missed the kick at goal.

Just before half-time, however, Messenger, the Australian captain, finished off a fine passing move to touch down and make the score 5–3 to the tourists. After the break, brilliant work by Fish, George Dickenson and Ike Taylor took play to the Australian line where, following a scrum, Messenger relieved the pressure with a huge kick. More fine play by Fish sent Dickenson racing to the posts, but the referee ruled that the pass had been forward. It was a close call and a controversial decision and the crowd groaned in disappointment.

George Thomas levelled the scores with a penalty and Warrington attacked again; Welsh forward Billy O'Neill sent Fish on a thrilling run to the line. Again the kick was missed, but Warrington still led 8–5 as the game entered its final stages before Messenger again intervened.

The Australian captain raced clear of the Warrington defence and passed to Frawley, who crossed at the corner to make the score 8–8. More controversy followed. The Australians claimed that Frawley, who had not been tackled, had not touched down in the corner; he had only pretended to do so to trick Fish, before running behind the posts and touching down there. The referee, however, awarded the try in the corner, despite Australian protests. Still, Messenger had the chance to win the match for the Kangaroos with a kick from the touchline, but his brave attempt missed by a yard.

7. Missing out on the 1910 tour

"Fish is still the best left wing in the Union when the mood takes him."

Jack Fish was in his prime as a try scorer for the four seasons from 1906–07 to 1909–10, from the ages of 27 to 31, during which his strike rate was almost one per match.

Season	Apps	Tries	Goals	Points
1906–07	24	24	38	148
1907-08	26	25	13	101
1908-09	33	26	44	166
1909-10	29	28	22	128
TOTALS	112	103	117	543

All he had to show for his efforts, however, in trophy terms at least, was the Challenge Cup winners' medal from 1907 when, as captain, he scored one try, created another and kicked four goals. But even Fish could not win every match, every week, on his own and the Warrington committee tried to build a team around him, by signing international players from Wales and Australia.

One of the driving forces behind this player recruitment was Harry Ashton, the club secretary and former Warrington forward. Ashton had been the team captain in April 1886 when the Wirepullers had won their first trophy, the South West Lancashire and Border Towns Cup, and was a powerful figure. He was also the landlord of the Roebuck Hotel in Bridge Street, Warrington, but, despite this, he was a strict disciplinarian and he banned Jack Fish – and the rest of the players – from drinking bottles of beer at half-time. They would have to make do with sliced lemons instead. Ashton's standing in the game is shown by the fact that he was elected president of the Northern Union for the 1907–08 season.

After winning the cup twice in the space of three seasons and reaching four finals in seven years, Ashton and the rest of the committee had set their hearts on winning the Northern Rugby League Championship for the first time in 1907-08 and the Wirepullers started the season like champions, with three comfortable victories, against Leigh, Rochdale Hornets and Runcorn.

The opening match against Leigh counted in three separate competitions – the West Lancashire League, the Lancashire League and the Northern Rugby League – and it only took Warrington two minutes to take control. Veteran centre Danny Isherwood created an opening for Fish and he beat two men to score and then kicked a huge conversion.

Warrington went on to win 28–3 while Fish went on to score 25 tries in 26 appearances and kick 13 goals for a seasonal haul of 101 points. Warrington's early promise faded, however, as they were undone by injuries and, in particular, their poor away form. The Wirepullers lost at St Helens, Broughton Rangers, Oldham, Hull, Runcorn, Leeds, Bradford and Wigan and drew at Widnes and Salford to finish seventh in the league table.

Still, Warrington were the Challenge Cup holders and to try to retain the trophy the committee made two major signings from Welsh rugby union in January 1908. Both men were 21 years old and so had youth on their side.

The Abertillery centre or winger Evan William Watkin was the first to arrive despite interest from Oldham, who were on top of the Lancashire League. Watkin had played union for Monmouthshire against Glamorgan, Yorkshire and Somerset and taken part in a Welsh trial game. At 5 feet 8 inches and 11 stones 6 pounds, he had already scored 23 tries for his club and six for his county that season.

He made his debut for Warrington 'A' against Egerton in the first round of the Lancashire Shield at Wilderspool on Saturday 18 January and marked the occasion with two of Warrington's 12 tries in a comfortable 46–0 victory. Two more tries followed in his second 'A' team appearance.

The Newport forward F.G. Jenkins arrived at Wilderspool later in the month. A blacksmith by trade, he was 5 feet 11 inches and 13 stone and had been a reserve for Wales against England and Scotland. He was catapulted straight into the first team and made his debut against Broughton Rangers at Wilderspool on 25 January. He impressed watching supporters and journalists.

The Broughton match was another first for the club as it was the first benefit match in Warrington's history with the fortunate player, the veteran centre Danny Isherwood, keeping all the gate receipts after the costs of staging the match had been deducted. A crowd of 6,622 turned out to honour him and Isherwood was later presented with £165 which in today's money would be £16,500.

Fittingly, Isherwood scored the only try, taking a pass from Ernie Brookes to cross at the posts, as Warrington won 5–2. Isherwood, whose father had played for the club, had been signed from the Stockton Heath rugby club, also known as the Heathens.

Victory at Wigan in February would have given Warrington the West Lancashire Championship but, despite another try from Fish, the Wirepullers lost 11–5.

The return fixture was at Wilderspool one week later and Wigan were lifted by the presence of New Zealander Lance Todd at centre, after he had been signed following the All Golds tour. However,

60

Warrington achieved a brilliant 14–3 victory; winger Evan Watkin scored his first try for the first team.

All eyes were now on the Challenge Cup; Warrington safely dispatched Halifax in the first round at Wilderspool in front of a crowd of 8,000 to earn a second round visit to Runcorn.

This tie attracted a crowd of 10,000 – including 4,000 from Warrington – and the Wirepullers won 6–2 thanks to tries from Fish and Ike Taylor. Watkin, however, had caused some anxious moments with his suspect defence and he was dropped for the next two games.

Warrington travelled to Broughton Rangers in the third round for a match that attracted a huge crowd of 21,275 – including 5,000 from Warrington, many of whom travelled on special trains. The Wirepullers, however, lost F.G. Jenkins through injury early on, reducing them to 12 men, and crashed to a 7–2 defeat at Wheater's Field.

The season was all but over, but Warrington's 'A' team were still in the Lancashire Shield and because Fish had missed the Lancashire Cup games earlier in the season he was eligible to play. Fish crossed for four tries in the semi-final against Radcliffe Rangers, despite some muted protests from the visitors that his inclusion wasn't really fair. He also played in the final against Wigan 'A' at Central Park where Wigan, who fielded some 'ringers' themselves, including Lance Todd, ran out 19–6 winners in front of 7,000 supporters.

To try to spread the Northern Union game into London, Warrington played Wakefield Trinity at West Ham on Saturday 18 April with a silver cup on offer to the winners. A fair crowd turned out to watch the action with Warrington losing 11–6. Jack Cartwright and Ernie Jordan scored the Warrington tries – one in each half – and the play was described as "fast and exciting" but the game did not lead to a Northern Union boom in London. Fish played brilliantly but, for once, did not score.

Two Welsh teams, Merthyr Tydfil and Ebbw Vale, had joined the Northern League for the 1907–08 season and this led to the first England versus Wales international match being staged at Tonypandy on Easter Monday 1908 in front of a promising crowd of 12,000. Again, Fish was part of history as the teams lined up as follows:

Wales: T. Jenkins (Ebbw Vale), L. Treharne (Wigan), B. Jenkins (Wigan),
P. Thomas (Leeds), D. Thomas (Halifax), R. Rees (Merthyr Tydfil), J. Thomas (Wigan), A. Buckler (Salford), G. Ruddick (Broughton Rangers), D. Jones (Merthyr Tydfil), D.B. Davies (Merthyr Tydfil), O. Burgham (Ebbw Vale),
J. Saunders (Ebbw Vale).
England: W.H. Taylor (Hull), J. Fish (Warrington), G. Dickenson (Warrington),
A. Hogg (Broughton Rangers), W. Batten (Hunslet), J. Jolley (Runcorn),
T. White (Oldham), J. Spenser (Salford), W. Holder (Hull), J.W. Birch (Leeds),
R. Padbury (Runcorn), A. Robinson (Halifax), S. Warwick (Salford).
Referee: R. Robinson (Bradford).

Wales won 35–18, but Fish was the best player on view. He scored two tries and kicked two goals for the defeated England team in what was his last representative appearance. George Dickenson, his regular centre with Warrington, fulfilled the same role for England, but it was the Wigan trio of winger Lewis Treharne, centre Bert Jenkins and scrum-half Johnny Thomas who won the game for Wales. Treharne and Jenkins scored two tries apiece while Thomas kicked seven goals.

The season ended on a sad note, however, with the sudden death of the former Warrington forward and committee member James T. 'Tosh' Thorniley, the man who had discovered Fish, following a heart attack. Thorniley, aged just 41, left a widow and seven children and, because his death was so unexpected, he had made no provision for them. The club stepped in with a hardship grant.

The annual general meeting was held at the Co-operative Hall in Cairo Street at the end of May when Alderman David Tinnion, a former player, was elected president in succession to Ted Warren, another former player.

Following the success of the All Golds tour and the first Anglo-Welsh international, optimism was in the air and the outgoing president predicted that within four or five years the Northern Union game would have replaced the Rugby Football Union game throughout England and Wales, with the exception of the public schools. His remarks were greeted with rapturous applause and nods of approval.

At the start of the 1908-09 season, Warrington signed two international forwards from Welsh rugby union: Billy Dowell, from Pontypool, in September, and Billy O'Neill, from Cardiff, in October. Dowell, aged 23, had previously played for Newport and had won seven caps from 1907-08. He was a solidly-built 6 feet tall and weighed 13 stone 7 pounds. O'Neill, aged 30, had won 11 caps from 1904 to 1908 and played in all of Wales's international matches the previous season. O'Neill was a line-out specialist, an excellent ball handler and had spent 10 seasons with Cardiff, making 208 appearances, and his decision to "go over" to the Northern Union caused consternation in the Valleys.

O'Neill defended himself, eloquently, in an interview in the *South Wales Daily News.* "I go," he said, "to better myself. I have a wife and child, and I am only a working man. I was offered £100 down, and I couldn't resist it – indeed I felt at the time and I now feel it too, that I would have failed in my duty to my wife and my young child if I had not taken the chance – it takes a working man a long time to save £100 you know. It may be all right for well-to-do people to say they prefer amateur sport – I have been satisfied with that myself until now – but let them put themselves in my position.

"My only regret is that I have to leave Cardiff, where I have many friends, and where I have received every kindness from the old club committee, officials and my fellow players. I had to wrestle with myself before I could put pen to paper to sign myself to go North because of the happy days I have spent in Cardiff, but we – my wife and I – think it was the best thing to do, and I hope my old football friends will try to place themselves in my position before condemning me."

To put O'Neill's decision to go north into a modern perspective, £100 in 1908 equates to £10,000 today. O'Neill and O'Dowell travelled up from South Wales together for Warrington matches, leaving Cardiff on Friday evening and returning on Saturday night or Sunday morning. O'Neill worked on Cardiff Docks for 56 years, and became a staff foreman and trade union delegate.

Jack Fish, meanwhile, was almost 30 years old and had problems with his weight. At the start of his career, he had tipped the scales at 11 and a half stones, but during the 1907–08 campaign he had ballooned to 13 and a half stones. Some reports even have him tipping the scales at 14 stones 4 pounds when he played for England against Wales on Easter Monday. Pre-season training in the summer of 1908 had seen him drop to 12 stones 8 pounds but, during the early weeks of the new season, his weight started to creep up again.

Eventually, the Warrington committee lost patience with him and he was dropped for the visit to Broughton Rangers on Saturday 24 October, along with centre Ike Taylor and forwards Alf and Peter Boardman, for "inattention to training". Warrington lost at Broughton and, with Fish still out of the team, only just sneaked past lowly Merthyr Tydfil 5–0 in a dour game at Wilderspool the following week.

This was not the all-action entertainment the Warrington public wanted and so Fish was recalled for the trip to St Helens in the first round of the Lancashire Cup on Saturday 7 November 1908 and showed the supporters – and the committee – exactly what they had been missing.

He scored three tries and had two other efforts disallowed for offside. He also kicked two goals and tormented John Manchester, the St Helens threequarter. He was also laid out following a knock on the head, but recovered to complete his hat-trick in the last 10 minutes with a brilliant try after apparently being surrounded.

This was more like it, although the rugby league writer in the *Warrington Examiner* was not entirely happy: "Fish is still the best left wing in the Union when the mood takes him and his feet are not clogged by inattention to training. If he would only get about 14 pounds of that superfluous fat off, he would soon be dazzling the eye of the crowd as of yore.

"It was remarkable how well he ran on Saturday, and to score three tries was no mean feat. As a matter of fact, he crossed the St Helens line on five occasions, twice being adjudged off-side and the way he ran rings around Manchester didn't half suit the local enthusiasts.

"If Jack will just make the necessary effort he will earn further honours and perhaps get the benefit which he had almost forfeited his claim to. Even the New Zealand trip is not out of his reach. All he has to do is cast a smaller shadow when the sun shines, and score a try or two each week."

The try-scoring part, at least, was almost second nature and the following week Fish scored a try against the Kangaroos – described in Chapter Six – before scoring again at Swinton in the second round of the Lancashire Cup to help earn Warrington a 6–2 victory and a semi-final against Wigan.

Wigan were the team that everyone was talking about and the conversation was not always flattering. In October 1908, Edward Croston, a coal dealer from Whelley, near Wigan, was charged with "unlawfully and corruptly" attempting to bribe two Wigan players, the New Zealanders Lance Todd and William 'Massa' Johnston, to lose a match against Hunslet.

At the trial in Wigan in November, the court heard that Croston had been seen talking to the two players at the club's headquarters, the Dog and Partridge pub, on the evening of 10 September. He later placed a bet of 21 shillings, about £400 in today's money, on Hunslet to win the following Saturday.

Wigan won 18–10. Croston was convicted and sent to jail for two months with hard labour. The Northern Union congratulated Wigan on their handling of the case and banned Croston from every game within their jurisdiction.

Wigan's Lancashire Cup second round tie with Leigh was also cloaked in controversy. The tie ended in a 3–3 draw at Leigh before Wigan won the replay at Central Park 11–5. Leigh objected to the result on the grounds that 'Massa' Johnston had left the field to change his jersey without first obtaining the permission of the referee.

The Lancashire County Union upheld the objection and said that the referee had committed a great error of judgment in allowing Johnston to continue to take further part in the game. The replay was ordered to be replayed and again Wigan won, this time 17–3.

After this, all roads led to Central Park for the semi-final on Saturday 5 December when a crowd of 19,000 assembled to watch two of Lancashire's finest sides do battle. Wigan were at full strength while Warrington were missing stand-off Ernie Brookes with a knee injury.

Fish always loved the big stage and it did not take him long to show that he was still one of the most resourceful players in the Union. After good work by Jack Lloyd, Jack Jenkins, Ike Taylor and George Dickenson, the great winger hurled himself at the Wigan line, injuring himself in the process, to give Warrington a 3–0 lead. Dickenson missed the kick and Wigan replied with two tries from winger Jimmy Leytham, the second of which was converted by full-back Jim Sharrock to give them an 8–3 lead at half-time.

A Fred Gleave try, again converted by Sharrock, stretched Wigan's lead to 13–3, but Warrington were far from finished. Fish was obstructed and kicked the resulting penalty himself to narrow the gap. Scrum-half Jack Jenkins then scored a second Warrington try, converted by Fish, to make the score 13–10 and worry Wigan. Still, Warrington attacked before Sharrock kicked a penalty goal to make the final score 15–10 at the end of a marvellous contest.

After that, Warrington's hopes of a successful season rested on a decent Challenge Cup run, especially after they were drawn at home to mid-table Leeds in the first round. It was a match they were expected to win – and win comfortably – and, inevitably, complacency set in.

Four days before the cup tie, on Shrove Tuesday, Warrington had a rearranged league match at Halifax. The Warrington committee decided that it was not necessary to rest any key players and, again inevitably, two of Warrington's three best backs – centre George Dickenson and stand-off Ernie Brookes – were injured in a 23–8 defeat, which ruled them out of the cup tie. Still, Warrington could count on Jack Fish, or could they?

That week, for one week only, the new Palace and Hippodrome Theatre at Friars Gate in Warrington – which had been opened in 1907 and is now the Showroom nightclub – was staging Fred Karno's production of his "colossal" show called *The Football Match*.

Written by Fred Karno, who had discovered Charlie Chaplin, and Fred Kitchen, the show followed the fortunes of Midnight Wanderers and Middleton Pie-cans with leading actor Harry Weldon playing the part of "Stiffy" the goalkeeper. Playing to packed houses, there were two performances per night – at 7pm and 9pm – and admission prices ranged from 3d in the gallery to 6d in the pit and 1s in the circle. The show also featured a "host of stars" including:
Hicks and Hunter, vocalists and ice skate dancers; Harvey and Holt, comedy speciality artistes; Decima Brook, dainty comedian and dancer; Walker and May, coloured vocalists, featuring Walker, the only blind comedian in the world; Elton and Edwin, the world's premier banjoists; Raymond's bio tableaux; Sisters Hampel, the comedy couple; and Cestria, the comedy juggler and acrobatic waiter.

On the Thursday afternoon, two days before the Challenge Cup tie against Leeds, Fred Karno's company organised a charity football match and asked Jack Fish, the town's leading sportsman, to take part.

Fish agreed, but the stage was set for disaster and the winger suffered a badly sprained ankle, which ruled him out of the cup tie as well. Warrington supporters were furious when they found out.

The cup game was 0–0 at half-time before Leeds ran out 5–3 winners; centre Ike Taylor scored the Warrington try. The town of Warrington was said to be in a state of shock that Saturday night as the dreams of further Challenge Cup glory disappeared. To make matters worse, Leeds lost to Hunslet in the next round.

Effectively, Warrington's season was over, but they were determined to finish the campaign in style. Bradford Northern visited Wilderspool for a friendly on March 13 and were dispatched 30–3 with Taylor and George Thomas scoring two tries apiece. Swinton were thrashed 36–6 – Warrington's then highest score against the Lions – with Thomas scoring two tries and kicking six goals.

Finally, on Easter Monday 1909, Warrington annihilated St Helens by a then club record 78–6, and scored 20 tries with nine goals in the process. St Helens arrived with a weakened team and then lost a player with a broken leg, which reduced them to 12 men.

In front of 3,000 supporters, Warrington took full advantage and led 40–0 at half-time. By the end, two Warrington players – winger Bert Bradshaw and Welsh forward George Thomas – had scored five tries apiece, equalling Jack Fish's club record against Goole in March 1900.

Thomas also kicked eight goals – seven conversions and one from a mark – for a then club record haul of 31 points, beating the 30 points Fish had scored against Huddersfield at Wilderspool in October 1906. Thomas's record stood for more than 90 years until Lee Briers bagged 40 points (three tries and 14 goals) in a Challenge Cup tie against York – also at Wilderspool – in February 2000.

Warrington's 78 points was also a record – beating the 59 points scored against Rugby (10 goals and three tries) in the rugby union days of December 1893. That record, too, would stand until the Challenge Cup tie against York which Warrington won 84–1.

Although overshadowed on the day, Fish still scored a try and kicked a goal to take his seasonal tally to 26 tries and 44 goals for a grand total of 166 points – yet another club record.

Five days later, with Fish again injured, Warrington closed their season at Rochdale, as they had opened it at Leigh back in September, with a 6–5 defeat. This led to an unhappy annual meeting at the Bold Street Wesleyan Schoolroom at the end of May. The members told the committee to spend more money on players, because it would be recouped by more supporters paying to attend matches. Tony Davies, for the committee, replied that signing players was not as easy as plucking blackberries in September.

King Edward VII and Queen Alexandria made a flying visit to Warrington on Tuesday 6 July 1909 – the first to the town by a reigning monarch for almost 100 years. Their majesties stopped at Warrington Town Hall – on their way from Worsley in Manchester to Waterloo in Liverpool – where there was a three-minute civic ceremony. The royal couple never once got out of their car, however, and so the thousands of townsfolk who lined the streets barely caught a glimpse of them.

The royal visit was recorded at length in the local papers on Saturday 10 July. Just as interesting, for Warrington supporters at least, was the news in the same editions that Warrington FC had signed two of the Kangaroos – Larry O'Malley, the auburn-haired forward, and Dan Frawley, the big right winger.

O'Malley, aged 25, was 5 feet 10 inches tall and weighed 11 stone 5 pounds, which was on the light side for a forward, but he was very fast. Frawley, aged 24, was the same height as his fellow countryman and weighed 11 stones 10 pounds, which made him a powerful threequarter.

Before leaving Australia, both had played for New South Wales versus New Zealand in Sydney on Saturday 5 June, when New South Wales, captained by O'Malley, won 26–21. Frawley played centre to winger Albert Rosenfeld and the pair tore New Zealand apart with their pace and inter-passing.

Frawley and Rosenfeld, who had signed for Huddersfield, travelled to England together. Frawley arrived in Warrington on Thursday 12 August, in plenty of time for the start of the new season.

Unfortunately, he injured an ankle in his first practice match. Initially, the problem was thought to be just a sprain, but further investigation revealed a broken bone and he ended up on crutches for a month before finally making his first-team debut at home to Broughton Rangers in October.

O'Malley arrived in England on Saturday 4 September, feeling fit and ready for action and made his debut at Rochdale seven days later, which made him the first Australian to play for the club. O'Malley showed dash, speed and resourcefulness as Warrington won 9–6.

Still, the Warrington committee had not finished their spending spree and they also tried to sign 'The Master', Dally Messenger, and forward Chas Pierce, two more of the Kangaroos touring team.

Sadly, Messenger had a knee injury and his doctor advised him not to sign and Pearce would not travel from Australia without him. Messenger, however, recommended that Warrington sign winger John Stuntz instead and the committee agreed.

Stuntz had not been one of the Kangaroos, but had subsequently played for Australia against the Maoris and scored tries galore, including four on his debut for Eastern Suburbs in 1908, which is still an Australian record. Aged 23, Stuntz – who was known as Johnno in Australia, but was called Jim in England – was frighteningly quick, having run 120-yard handicap races back home in 12 seconds.

Warrington had to pay a transfer fee of £125 – about £12,500 in today's money – while Stuntz was paid £3 5s per week. He was 5 feet 7 inches tall and weighed 11 stones 7 pounds.

Warrington cabled the money to Australia and Stuntz boarded a steamship bound for England. He arrived at Bank Quay Station on 22 November where he was greeted by 800 Warrington fans. He made his debut a few days later for Warrington's 'A' team against Cadishead at Wilderspool where 6,000 supporters were amazed by his pace. He marked his first team debut against Hull at Wilderspool the following week with a try, and touched down with a flamboyant dive.

Unfortunately, Stuntz had also agreed to play some games for Barrow, in direct contravention of Northern Union rules, and was fined £25 by the union for his mistake.

Not surprisingly, with all this transfer activity going on, interest in the club was at an all-time high and the 8,000 crowd against Leigh in September was the biggest opening day attendance in the club's history.

Warrington made an excellent start to the season and the 19–0 victory at Widnes in September took them to the top of the Northern Rugby League table for the first time in the club's history, although Warrington only held top spot for 58 hours, until they lost 10–2 to Huddersfield at Fartown in front of 12,000 supporters.

Warrington regained top spot with a 27–13 victory over Broughton Rangers at Wilderspool on a vile day in October when Jack Fish scored two tries. His second was a magnificent effort as the winger evaded half the Rangers team on his way to the line.

"The climax was reached in the second half when Fish obliged with what was really his masterpiece of the season," purred the *Warrington Guardian*. "It appeared almost impossible for him to escape the clutches of at least half-a-dozen of the Rangers, but the manoeuvring of the feet was so cleverly accomplished that Fish appeared to have a charmed existence, and when he finally cleared Barlow (the Rangers full-back) with the grace of a finished player the crowd let go their pent-up appreciation in a manner which made the welkin ring. Yes, it was a magnificent try and worthy to rank among the many brilliant ones Fish has recorded in a primrose and blue jersey."

Fish was in sensational form. From 11 September to 30 October, he scored points in nine consecutive matches, notched up 13 tries and four goals. In November, Merthyr Tydfil arrived at Wilderspool late and with only 12 players. Fish punished them to the tune of 24 points, with four tries and six goals. By Christmas Eve, Fish had played in all 16 matches, scored 22 tries and kicked 15 goals for a total of 118 points.

Things started to go wrong on Christmas Day when Warrington were held to a 0–0 draw at Leigh. Two days later, they lost 8–0 at home to Rochdale Hornets. Then, to make matters much worse, Fish suffered a bad leg injury against Wigan at Wilderspool on 3 January 1910. The flying winger was never quite the same player again, even though he finished the season with a club record 28 tries, and the injury almost certainly cost him a place on the first Northern Union tour to Australia and New Zealand at the end of the season.

The Wigan match was accompanied by amazing scenes: 11,146 supporters paid at the turnstiles and about 1,100 of the club's 1,200 members were also present. Then, shortly before kick-off, about 2,500 Wigan supporters pushed through the gates on the popular side of the ground, which took the total attendance to more than 14,000.

Before he was injured, Fish had kicked a penalty goal and raced over for a try in the corner and Warrington, with an excellent team performance, held on to win 8–6.

Without Fish and missing him at his best in the months ahead, however, Warrington's form faded and they eventually finished seventh in the Northern Rugby League table. A poem from the time stresses his importance to the team.

Stuntz can run, and then he's done
Catch a ball and that is all
Geo Dicky is very tricky
Very light and tall
Brookes looks fine
When he is bound for the line
But I would rather see Fish on
When he is in condition
The lad can beat them all

The Challenge Cup still generated excitement in the town with Warrington having the luck of the draw and home victories over Wigan Highfield, Millom and Hunslet earning the Wirepullers a place in the semi-finals.

The semi-final was against Leeds at Wheater's Field, Broughton and 4,000 Warrington fans made the journey on 2 April to see their heroes in action. Fish was still injured and in his place the committee selected 20-year-old Will McIntyre, who had been signed from the Stockton Heath club.

Warrington made a poor start and were trailing 11–0 after 20 minutes before a try from centre George Dickenson made the half-time score 11–3. After the break, McIntyre scored a try – his first for the club – and kicked two goals to cut the deficit to one point. But that was how the score remained. Warrington had lost 11–10 and were out of the cup.

Following that disappointment, Warrington suffered two bad defeats – 32–0 at home to Oldham and, embarrassingly, 13–6 at Merthyr Tydfil. A season that had started with such optimism had delivered just the West Lancashire Cup, based on the mini league featuring Warrington, Wigan, St Helens, Leigh, Widnes and Runcorn. Warrington had achieved two 0–0 draws with Leigh and six wins from the other eight matches.

For one Warrington player, however, the season was far from over because burly Welsh forward Frank Shugars had been selected for the first Northern Union tour. In March, the Warrington committee had nominated six players for the trip – Fish, stand-off Ernie Brookes, scrum-half Jack Jenkins and Welsh forwards Billy O'Neill, George Thomas and Shugars. Between them, the 27 Northern Union clubs nominated 150 players.

Shugars, however, was the only Warrington player to be selected for one of the two trial matches. Fish was delighted that his friend was going on tour, but bitterly disappointed not to be making the trip of a lifetime himself, a disappointment that was shared by many supporters in Sydney.

A large party of well-wishers gathered at Warrington's Central Station on Thursday 14 April to see Shugars off on the train to Manchester where a farewell dinner was to be held at the Grosvenor Hotel. A local testimonial fund to help him on his way had raised £15 and been used to buy a trunk full of items: a suit, a deck suit, three pairs of pyjamas, flannel and cotton shirts, under vests, six pairs of socks, two dozen linen collars, one dozen flannel collars, two dozen handkerchiefs, shoes, sweater, cap, slippers, deck boots, nine ties, cuff links, seven collar pins, safety razor, hair brush, clothes brush and comb.

The players who saw him off at the station – including Jack Fish – presented him with a silver-mounted pipe. People in his hometown of Tonypandy had also clubbed together and presented him with a gold watch in appreciation of him being chosen for the tour.

The tour was an epic adventure that began when the party sailed from Tilbury on 15 April and did not end until the tourists arrived back at Plymouth on 16 September – five months later. Shugars collected his only Northern Union cap during the trip when he played against New Zealand in Auckland on 30 July. The Northern Union won 52–20. When, finally, he arrived back in Warrington he admitted that he had had a "ripping" time.

Another member of that first Great Britain touring party was the 20-year-old Hunslet centre or winger Billy Batten. On 30 November 1910, completely out of the blue, Warrington received a telegram from Hunslet saying that Batten was for sale for the world record fee of £400, about £100,000 in today's money.

The Warrington committee decided to offer Hunslet just £200 and the Yorkshire club were not interested. Two years later, however, they sold Batten to Hull for the world record sum of £600. With hindsight, Batten would have been a worthy successor to Fish in the Warrington team. He was a brilliant athlete and a huge crowd puller. He became famous for his trademark "Batten Leap" – his remarkable ability to hurdle players who were attempting to tackle him. It would have been £400 well spent.

Warrington were, however, moving with the times and also in 1910 the first telephone was installed at Wilderspool, with the number Warrington 155. By 1971, that number had grown to Warrington 35338. By 2010 callers had to dial 0871 622 1879.

Throughout south west Lancashire and beyond, Jack Fish was a sporting celebrity and he became friends with a celebrity from another walk of life – the comedian George Formby senior. Formby was three years older than Fish, having been born in Ashton-Under-Lyne in 1875, and enjoyed an even more remarkable rags-to-riches success story, taking him from singing in the rough pubs of Wigan to performing at the London Palladium.

His journey also took him from absolute poverty and sleeping in doorways to owning a magnificent house, Hillcrest, now a listed building, on London Road, Stockton Heath, a mile or so from Fish's more humble abode. When Formby died from tuberculosis, aged just 45, in February 1921 he left more than £21,000, which translates to more than £1million today, and a son, the ukulele playing George Formby junior, who would become the country's highest-paid entertainer in the 1930s.

Formby senior was born as James Booth, the illegitimate son of an illiterate working-class mother, Sarah Jane Booth. Some months after his birth, his mother married his father, Francis Lawler, but the marriage turned out to be turbulent and violent. Young James was often ill-treated and not given enough to eat and, in later life, he observed: "My childhood was the most miserable that could have happened to any human being."

The George Formby Senior website takes up the story: "Not surprisingly, James Booth ran away from home at the earliest opportunity, and as a lad of 13, started his stage career in the rough pubs and ale-houses around Wigan, as the soprano half of 'The Brothers Glenray – the songbirds of the Music Halls'.

"For three years the duo made a meagre living by singing sentimental tear-jerkers to the hard audiences of the Midlands and the North. By 1892, The Brothers Glenray had escaped from tap-rooms and free and easies and were now appearing in real music halls – far from the top of the bill, but none the less, in regular work, until their voices started to break and they got more laughter than applause for their vocal harmonies.

"As audiences seemed determined to laugh at him, James Booth decided that they might as well laugh with him, so The Brothers Glenray parted and he adopted a folio of comic songs adapted from Methodist hymn tunes, grotesque stage make-up, and a new name.

"The name came to him while he was seated on a draughty railway platform waiting for a train to take him to his next engagement. He idly noticed a goods train passing on the opposite platform, with the wagons labelled to FORMBY. He liked the name and 'George Formby' he became until his death 24 years later.

"At first, bookings were few, but George Formby gradually built up a following as a droll, dry comedian. His material was simple and he had four or five basic costumes, all more or less clown-like, and in between songs he would do little more than come to the front of the stage to chat to the stalls as if talking over a pint in the bar of the local pub. His personality was engaging and audiences loved him.

"In 1899, George met and married Eliza Hoy, who became the mainstay of his life. She encouraged him to keep on trying whenever he got depressed; supported their young family by dressmaking when bookings were low; and provided a happy and fulfilled family background. Liza was just the prop he needed to go outside the provinces and attack the big managements in London."

Formby first appeared in London in about 1900 and was an overnight success, with audiences loving his portrayal of a simple northerner. He would often open his act with: "Good Evening. I'm Formby from Wigan. I've not been in England long." And his clowning influenced another would-be performer, the young Charlie Chaplin.

It is not entirely clear when Fish and Formby first met, but the latter must have performed many times at the theatres in Warrington, even before he moved his entire family to Stockton Heath around about the time of the First World War. Mr and Mrs Formby had 12 children, seven of whom survived infancy, the eldest of whom, George junior, was born in Wigan in 1904. Fish's eldest surviving child, Alice, was born in Warrington in 1903. Fish and Formby had much in common.

Yet the years of poverty and neglect had left Formby with a harsh, rasping cough, which he would work into his act whenever he had an attack on stage. "I'm coughin' better tonight," he would say and plug his favourite patent medicine 'Zambuk' – long before the days of the National Health Service.

At other times he would explain it away as: "It's not the coughin' that carries you off it's the coffin they carry you off in!" The audiences loved it, not realising that Formby was already terminally ill.

While playing in pantomime in 1918 and 1919, he had to leave the cast because of his agonising chest complaint. He usually managed to return, but during a performance in Newcastle upon Tyne in the 1920-21 season, he collapsed on stage.

His wife took him back home to Hillcrest, but despite her careful nursing, he died on Shrove Tuesday, 8 February, 1921 and was buried in Warrington Cemetery. George junior immediately abandoned his chosen career as a jockey and followed in his father's footsteps, even using his material.

Formby senior was much imitated and after Warrington won the Lancashire Cup for the first time in December 1921, Jack Prescott, the Wire captain, performed his impressions of the ground-breaking entertainer at the celebration dinner at the Kings Cafe in Bridge Street, Warrington.

1910 Warrington team: Back: J. Waywell, I. Taylor, J.W. Chesters, F. Green, H. McIntyre, J.H. Tilley; middle: G. Dickenson, W. Morgan, G. Thomas, J. Polson, A. Naylor; front: J. Benjamin, J. Fish, J. Jenkins.

8. For the benefit of Mr Fish

"Brilliant in attack, safe and reliable on the defence, he could also tackle, kick with either foot equally well, and was a model of consistency."

To thank Jack Fish for a dozen years of outstanding service to the club, the Warrington committee awarded him a testimonial match. Fish could keep the profits from any home fixture in the 1910–11 season, except the Wigan game on 12 November and the holiday matches against Leigh on Boxing Day and Runcorn on 2 January. The club was counting on big attendances at those matches to help to balance the books.

Fish agonised over the decision and eventually narrowed the choice down to two games, the visit of Oldham on 22 October and the visit of St Helens on 17 December. Finally, he picked the Oldham match, although at the start of the season it was by no means certain that he would be able to play in it.

Fish scored some tries in the pre-season practice matches but clearly was not fit. Everyone could see he was struggling and some supporters were even poking fun at him, perhaps in a good natured way, perhaps not.

Journalist George Archer, writing in the *Warrington Observer* newspaper, was outraged: "He [Fish] was out on Tuesday night but was too spasmodic and evidently cannot maintain the pace yet. I was surprised that many on the reserved side showed bad taste when the famous player was compelled to retire owing to nature failing him.

"For twelve good years Fish has been the one bright ornament of the club and it is impossible to estimate how valuable an asset he has been. I have always been led to believe that in the declining days of fame it is always the rule to extend sympathy not ridicule."

Luckily for Fish the committee had decided that a professional trainer was needed to prepare the first and 'A' teams for matches and so they placed an advertisement in various publications: "Wanted, an experienced man to train a football team; must be a good manager, steady, reliable."

The advert did the trick and in September Warrington appointed Fred Paley, a former professional sprinter from Sheffield, who had been training teams for two decades. His CV included Carlisle United, Newton Heath (before they became Manchester United in 1902), Port Vale, Arsenal and Reading. Paley's strict training regime involved sprinting, long walks, dumb-bell lifting, skipping, punch ball and baths.

His first task was to get Fish fit for his big day and, after only a few sessions, the winger was picked for the trip to Runcorn on Saturday 8 October. Warrington won 22–3 and Fish, though still overweight, just about got through the 80 minutes. Seven days later, against Broughton Rangers at Wilderspool, he was even more like his old self and, in the second half, he picked up a loose ball and forced his way over to help Warrington win 16–5.

In the build-up to the benefit match, tributes poured in. Mr W. McCutcheon, a well-known referee, described Fish as a "great Ruggerite". He continued: "A brainy, polished and gentlemanly player, endowed with wonderful dodging and kicking powers, and one of the most feared and dangerous exponents of his day. Always a thorn in the side of his opponents and the cause of deep concern to referees, who never knew what fresh sensations would be the outcome of his being in possession of the ball.

"The Warrington club and supporters in particular, and the football-loving public in general, owe much to him for many thrilling performances, which will live in the memory of those who have been fortunate enough to witness the prowess on the field of this sterling player.

"He is, indeed, deserving of a bumper benefit as a just reward for the long, faithful and conspicuous service upon the triumph of a most remarkable career. Jack has my best wishes for a further run of success off the field, and may he prove as worthy a citizen as he demonstrated he was a player."

Another referee, Mr E.H. Smirk, said that Fish was "one of the best three-quarters that ever donned a Northern Union jersey. A dreaded opponent, but a grand player to have on one's side, as a score was always possible with Fish in possession of the ball, and he was a brilliant goal kicker in addition."

Frank Renton, Yorkshire's leading official, added: "In my capacity as a referee under the Northern Union rules, I sincerely say that Jack Fish is one of the finest threequarters who ever stepped on a field, and of the many notable incidents which came under my notice was the try he scored in the final tie against Oldham three years ago at Broughton. He intercepted a pass intended for an opponent, ran to the full-back, kicked over his head, regained possession and turned what looked a possible defeat into a victory. This is one of the many brilliant incidents I have noticed in a career brimful of interesting episodes."

Journalist E.J. Dromgoole, who used the pseudonym 'Philistine', said: "The names of Jack Fish and Warrington for some years were synonymous. He was the star of the team when victories were frequent and defeats rare. To his unrivalled dashing runs and football efficiency Warrington owe many triumphs, and his brilliant individuality had a splendid effect on a side that was not lacking in fine combination. Sometimes one man may upset any attempt at harmonic understanding among a back division, but that was never a fault of Fish.

"As a matter of fact, he was the apex of a culminating series of schemes which had the scoring of tries the prime object. To get the ball into the hands of Fish was the everlasting aim, for those assisting knew that once in those safe fingers, speed and dodging power would be used, as only a great player can utilize them.

"Fish was as expert as a footballer as he was quick as a sprinter, and his mental activity was as great an asset as his rapidity of progress. In his best days – for like all famous players he has his moods – he was the man to keep the enthusiast watching in a state of delirious excitement. His journeys to the goal line of his opponents were calculated to create a succession of thrilling sensations, and given half a chance he crowned those feelings of pleasure with the glowing rapture of triumph.

"The many valuable records which Fish has placed to his credit and that of his club, will be memorable while football history lasts. Great player as he is he cannot, however, fight Anno Domini and Anti-Antiphon. Though he may not be as fast as in other days, he is still of tremendous value on a side, for his experience and resourcefulness.

"His name is something to conjure with, and his deeds should act as a stimulant on every young player. Warrington have turned out many famous players during their long and honourable career, but it is safe to say that none will rank higher in association with the club's name than that of Jack Fish."

The Yorkshire rugby writer *'Old Ebor'* compared Fish to Frank Ritchie, the former Bradford and Yorkshire winger and sprinter who had won more than £1,000 on the track, and Jack Dyson, the powerful Huddersfield threequarter who had won four caps for the England rugby union team from 1890 to 1892, and suggested that sometimes he had been too brave for his own good.

"John Fish was the Frank Ritchie and Jack Dyson of Northern Union football. Strong, fast, fearless but too much given to frontal attacks. Like Ritchie and Dyson, he went straight for his man, relying on strength and speed to send the would-be tackler into the touch gutter. This may have been bad for the other fellow but was not always good for Fish. A dodge or a flank movement would have saved him many a sore bone.

"One of the best tries I saw him get was in the Cup final against Oldham at Broughton three years ago. Under a united regime, Fish would have been a rugby international. No one would have enjoyed his robustiousness more than Rugby Unionists of the older school."

George Kilner, the Oldham secretary, wrote: "I have been with the Oldham club for eleven seasons, and I can honestly say that Jack Fish has, during that period, been one of the most popular visiting players at Watersheddings. He has given 'Owdham' many a nasty knock but that only tended to increase his popularity amongst the Oldham followers.

"Fish has always tried to play the game in a true sporting spirit. He has been a model on the field which any player might with advantage copy. His geniality has been on a par with his prowess and one regrets that his years have passed so quickly.

"Still the popular Fish may yet go on swimmingly for a long time. May he have, as he deserves to have, a bumping benefit − and may Oldham win!"

J.H. Houghton, the Lancashire secretary, said: "I always regarded Jack Fish as one of the smartest and best threequarters which the rugby world has ever known. It was a matter of much regret to the Colonials − especially the Sydney crowd − that Fish was not included in the team which recently visited Australasia, his career as a player having been followed very closely in the Antipodes. I hope that he will have a benefit deserving of his career."

Salford centre James Lomas, who had captained the first Northern Union team to tour Australia and New Zealand, wrote: "I have played with Jack Fish in county and international matches on many occasions and I think him the finest individual wing man who ever donned a jersey. The Lancashire team was never complete without him when he was at his best and that county owes a lot to him for their many successes.

"His services must have been invaluable to Warrington. I notice that he has again started playing and hope by the time his benefit comes round he will have found his true form.

"Fish's brilliant performances on the field are too well known for me to remind your readers, but I must say that his wonderful swerving and dodging, which were great characteristics peculiarly his own, have affected the downfall of many a team.

"Fish is well respected off the field. I wish him every success and hope he has a bumping benefit which he thoroughly deserves."

G.H. Marsden, the Bradford captain, added: "I have very good reasons for remembering Jack Fish, as on nearly all the occasions he played against Bradford he managed to score brilliant tries and was largely instrumental in the success of Warrington over our team; the third round of the NU Cup ties in 1900, and the semi-finals of 1904 and 1905 being the most noticeable.

"In the latter game he intercepted a pass in the first few minutes of the game, ran half the length of the field, and scored a brilliant try behind the posts, thus paving the way to victory for his side. I also remember him scoring a similar try in a Lancashire versus Yorkshire match at Oldham in 1904.

"Taken all round I regard Jack Fish as one of the best wing three-quarters I ever saw. Brilliant in attack, safe and reliable on the defence, he could also tackle, kick with either foot equally well, and was a model of consistency. Being stylish withal he was always a treat to watch, and always played a clean and gentlemanly game. I wish him a successful benefit."

Joe Riley, the Halifax captain, agreed and praised Fish's ability to side-step. He wrote: "I consider Jack Fish the finest wing three-quarter I have ever seen. Combined with his marvellous speed he has a wonderful double both ways which is most difficult to stop.

"I have always felt that whenever the ball was in his hands there was the utmost danger of a try being scored against my side. It has been a pleasure to oppose him because he always plays a clean and sportsmanlike game. I wish him a bumper benefit."

James Leytham, the Wigan captain, added: "I must say that Jack Fish was one of the best players in the Northern Union. I have seen him play in many matches and he always played the game and was always a trier to win matches. I am sure he is deserving of all he gets for the services he has done for Warrington. All my club mates wish him every success with a bumping benefit."

Lawrence O'Malley, the first Australian to play for Warrington, said: "I have found Jack a thorough sport and a fair-minded one in every sense of the word. Convey to him my heartiest congratulations and I hope his benefit will prove a huge success and pray he will live long to enjoy the proceeds."

Sam Houghton, the former England rugby union full-back who had grown up in the same part of Runcorn as the Warrington winger, said that he would be at the benefit match and described Fish as "the greatest wing threequarter that ever played".

He added: "I only knew one man in anything like the same class as Fish. That was Frank Miles, the old Salford player, who was equally wonderful as a dodger, but perhaps not as fast as Jack. Jack troubled me more than any other man I ever met. If he once got away with the ball, the odds were 20 to one on his dodging you. The only way to deal with John was to make your big effort just as he made his. You had to grab him low and stick to him without any considering. It isn't much use tackling a man like that round the head."

Houghton concluded that Fish was still "wonderful, considering his weight. A most dangerous man still anywhere near the line. I wish the Australians could have seen him in his pomp."

Wattie Davies, Batley's famous three-quarter, added: "If a few lines from me can in any way improve Jack's benefit I am only too pleased to send them. I consider Jack one of the best wingers that the Northern Union has produced and I know of no other player who can so easily trick a full-back when on the run. I trust he will have a fine day and a bumper gate."

Harry Gifford, Barrow's Lancashire full-back, agreed: "I am pleased to write you a line or two concerning my old friend, Jack Fish. To do him justice I should require more than a line or two. Of course, he was doing doughty deeds before I took part in first class football, but I saw quite enough to convince me he was the most slippery and most difficult threequarter to stop I ever played against.

"I have no hesitation in affirming that Jack Fish was the most accomplished wing threequarter playing Northern Union football. That he may have a bumper benefit is the earnest wish of his pal, Harry Gifford."

Finally, Dai Davies, a Challenge Cup finalist with Fish in 1904 and 1905, wrote from Ebbw Vale, where he was playing for the local Northern Union team. "It is, indeed, a privilege you extend to me to give my tribute to one whom I co-operated with whilst I was a member of the Warrington team. To attempt to eulogize his merits would be trying to paint the lily.

"During the whole of my career as a player I have never come across Jack Fish's superior. He had all the attributes which make the class player: resourceful, exceedingly clever when the situations were most difficult, and withal a splendid fellow to meet on the field of play.

"In all the time Fish has been before the British public he has won the golden opinion of followers of the handling code, and I am voicing the sentiments of all here in Ebbw Vale when I hope his benefit will be worthy of the man. Warrington owe him much, and it is hoped that the townspeople will rise to the occasion."

Supporters arrived early for the testimonial match so as not to miss any of the action and were entertained by the Crosfield's band, who played *For he's a jolly good fellow* as Fish ran out on to the pitch. As it was a special occasion, Fish and both captains were introduced to the guest of honour, Sir Gilbert Greenall, the former Conservative MP and member of the famous brewing family, before kick-off.

With the bumper crowd of almost 10,000 cheering him on, Fish went close to scoring a couple of times in the first half but was thwarted on each occasion to leave the half-time score at 0–0.

Scrum-half Jack Lloyd scored the opening try but George Thomas, the new Warrington captain, missed the kick. Jack Waywell, the other Warrington winger, was then knocked out in a tackle and spent 15 minutes on the sidelines trying to regain his senses.

Next, Warrington were awarded a penalty kick and it was decided that Fish would take it. It was one he would have kicked easily when he was in his prime and playing regularly but, on this occasion, despite the crowd willing him on, he missed badly. Oldham later scored a try themselves, brushing the struggling Waywell aside, and the match finished as a 3–3 draw.

Fish kept his place in the side for the trip to Knowsley Road a week later and, in the first half, pouched a well-timed pass from George Dickenson to score his customary try against St Helens – it was his 24th touchdown in 22 appearances against the Saints.

In the second half, though, Fish was hurt in stopping Matt Creevey, the St Helens scrum-half, from scoring what looked like a certain try and had to leave the pitch for five minutes to recover.

Father Time was catching up with him, but he still knew how to have a good time and the following month Fish treated his team-mates to dinner at the Royal Oak Branch pub to thank them for helping to make his benefit match such a success. Former full-back Frank Heesom was the master of ceremonies and Welshman George Thomas, inevitably, organised the post-meal singing, which no doubt included *The yellow rose of Texas*, which was one of his favourites.

To sort out the formalities of his benefit match, Fish was invited to attend a special meeting of the Warrington committee on Wednesday, 16 November. It was just over 12 years since he had faced the same committee as a wide-eyed teenager and been persuaded to sign for the club by the sight of silver coins piled high in front of him.

Fish was told that his benefit match had produced a profit of £268 2s 11d (about £27,000 in today's prices) once the referee, touch judges and police had been paid. Fish was told that £200 would be invested on his behalf and £50 put in a local bank with the balance (£18 2s 11d) handed over to the player. Fish thanked the committee for their efforts in making the benefit match a success and promised that he would do all in his power for the continuing success of the club.

He was now almost 32, however, and rapidly approaching the end of his playing career. He would have to wait two months for his next appearance in a Warrington jersey – for the 'A' team against Oldham 'A' in the Lancashire Combination at Wilderspool on Saturday 28 January 1911.

Fish had been training hard and his mere presence attracted a crowd of 5,000 – double the number who would normally have attended a reserve team fixture – and gave the team confidence.

Percy Clare crossed in the corner to make the half-time score 3–0 to Warrington before Oldham levelled matters with a try of their own. Fish then intervened. Receiving a pass from Clare he beat two men and made for the line. Unusually, he was overtaken near the corner and surrounded by half-a-dozen Oldham defenders.

Somehow he managed to dodge clear and sent a long pass out to Peter Boardman, Alf's younger brother, who scored Warrington's second try. A drop-goal from Bill Harmer near the end sealed an 8–3 victory and sent the fans home happy.

Fish's performance earned him a recall to the first team for the Challenge Cup first round tie at Coventry on Saturday, 18 February and, once again, the magic of the cup, worked wonders and he scored a try – his 214th for the Wirepullers – in the left-hand corner after taking a pass from George Dickenson. George Thomas added the goal from a difficult angle and Warrington went on to win 18–10.

Overall, though, Fish had not impressed and the committee dropped him to the 'A' team for the Lancashire Combination game against Swinton 'A' at Wilderspool the following Saturday. After 12 years at the top, Fish knew this was the end and decided not to turn out for the reserves. His Warrington career was over, but before he could officially announce his retirement the committee had put him on the transfer list. It was a brutal end to a wonderful career and one that Brian Bevan would face 51 years later.

The 1911 Census was taken on the night of Sunday 2 April and found Fish living at 10 York Street, a dwelling with four rooms, which was his home for the rest of his life.

He is listed as Jack Fish, not John Fish, and is a 32-year-old range fitter. His wife, Fanny, is a year younger and they have an eight-year-old daughter, Alice. To make ends meet, they also had a lodger, a 24-year-old single man, Joseph Carr, who was a labourer with the testing department at the Richmond Stove Company.

Times were changing and the first global news story made headlines all around the world in April 1912: the sinking of the Titanic. Although the ship had been built in Belfast and set sail from Southampton, the tragedy was still keenly felt in Warrington.

The Titanic's captain, Edward Smith, had lived at The Poplars, Liverpool Road, Great Sankey for around five years at the end of the previous century and was still remembered by many neighbours for his quiet sincerity and geniality. Smith's wife, Eleanor, was from a well-established Warrington family, the Penningtons, who had worked Woodhead Farm in Winwick for four generations. The couple had married at Winwick Parish Church in 1887.

Mrs Smith spoke for all the grieving families when she said: "To my poor fellow sufferers. My heart overflows with grief for you all, and is laden with the sorrow that has been thrust upon us. May God be with us all."

The Titanic's maiden voyage to New York was to have been Captain Smith's last duty for the White Star company before he retired at the age of 62. He went down with the ship.

Following the outbreak of the First World War in August 1914, Fish immediately volunteered to join the Army to fight the Germans. He was attached to the King's Royal Rifles, one of the country's top regiments.

It was now more than three years since he had last pulled on a Warrington jersey, but such was his enduring popularity that lots of local lads followed his example, with the result that the King's Royal Rifles became known locally as "Fish's regiment". Now aged 35, Fish also showed that he had not lost his exceptional pace by winning the Aldershot Command Sprint Championship.

Fish was transferred to the Rifle Brigade and stationed at Bury, from where his extraordinary playing career would take one final twist. At a meeting in August 1915, Warrington's committee members decided unanimously not to take part in senior football for the rest of the war, thus ignoring the series of friendly matches that were being arranged for the season.

Oldham had decided to carry on regardless and, in February 1916, Fish came out of retirement – aged 37 – to play for them against the league leaders Leeds at Watersheddings, five years after his last match for Warrington. When Fish's life story was published in the *Warrington Examiner* in 1938 this was presented as another triumph whereby he "scored the try and kicked the goal by which Oldham won." Sadly, the truth is not quite so romantic: Oldham lost 14–10 and Fish, playing on the right wing, endured a difficult afternoon. The rugby league writer in the *Oldham Evening Chronicle*, who used the pseudonym 'Grasshopper', reported: "Time was when Jack Fish was a terror, and I have seen him beat Oldham himself more than once; but he cannot do it now, and he was not much help to them on this initial appearance in the Oldham side.

"The inclusion of Fish was an experiment and the reasons for it were more sentimental than substantial, for he has been out of the game for years, and was 'done' before that. Still it was believed that he had got his 'tummy' off and was in form, and as he was desirous of a game he was invited, but he was not the Fish who used to make Warrington feared. No, they can't come back."

Fish never played professionally again, but in the spring of 1917 a new chapter in his life began with the birth of a strong, healthy son, who the couple named John, after his famous father. Fish survived the war unscathed, but not all his former friends and team-mates were so fortunate. The Warrington club lost 11 current and former players during the conflict, headed by the former captain, Welshman George Thomas, who, like Fish, had appeared in four Challenge Cup finals and made more than 300 appearances for the first team. Fish always had the utmost respect for Thomas and often described him as "one of the best forwards that ever lived".

George Thomas

The club's full roll of honour is as follows:

Sergeant Howard Davis, of the Rifle Brigade, who died aged 27, on 31 July 1915. He had made 22 appearances for the first team between 1912 and 1915, scoring one try.

Private James Andrews, of the South Lancashire Regiment, who died on 10 August 1915. He had made 49 appearances for the first team between 1895 and 1900.

Rifleman James Berry, of the Rifle Brigade, who died aged 48, on 8 September 1915. He had played for the first team for about five years, mainly in the club's rugby union days.

Rifleman Joseph Oakes, of the Rifle Brigade, who died aged 31 on 25 September 1915. He was a former 'A' team player who had also played for the Runcorn and Cadishead clubs.

Private George Thomas, of the South Lancashire Regiment, who died aged 35, on Monday 3 July 1916. He had made 385 first team appearances, mainly playing alongside Fish, scoring 47 tries and kicking 198 goals.

Private John Stuntz, of the Australian Infantry, who died on Thursday 3 May 1917. He had scored 13 tries in 19 appearances during the 1909–10 season.

Private Stanley Young, of the Manchester Regiment, who died aged 29 on 18 April 1918. He had made 60 appearances from 1913 to 1915, scoring two tries.

Private John Cartwright, of the Welsh Guards, who died aged 34 on 3 May 1918, leaving a wife and five children. He had made 33 appearances for the first team from 1906 to 1910, scoring five tries.

Three more 'A' team players – Alex Brown, Dalby Newall and E.J. Burton – also perished, although less is known about exactly when and where they met their deaths.

Two more of Fish's regular team-mates – full-back Jimmy Tilley and forward Arthur 'Crack' Naylor – were seriously wounded. Tilley, who was a member of the Warrington team who won the Challenge Cup in 1907, was awarded the Distinguished Conduct Medal for gallantry in 1916 but lost his right eye in May 1918.

Naylor, a Challenge Cup winner in 1905 and 1907, was wounded in July 1917 when a sniper's bullet passed through his ear, neck and back. In a letter home he wrote: "I am glad to tell you that I am improving. The doctors say that I am a very lucky man to be living."

Naylor, who was with the Grenadier Guards and had already served in the Boer War, made a full recovery, living to the ripe old age of 72. Fish and Naylor were among the thousands present at Bridge Foot on Sunday 8 November 1925 for the unveiling of the Warrington War Memorial by Lieutenant General Sir Richard Butler, of the Western Command. The memorial bore the names of the 1,131 men and one woman who were killed during the Great War.

"This is a proud memorial, that stands here for all time," said the general. "At the same time, war memorials in stone are not enough. These men during the war all worked together for the common good, each doing his duty in his own sphere to the utmost, and gave their lives to bring peace and prosperity to this country; and the greatest memorial we can erect is that all should do the same in peace, and thus ensure that they have not died in vain."

A postcard of Jack Fish that was popular with Warrington supporters.

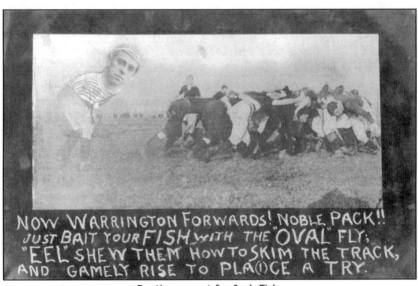
Poetic support for Jack Fish.

9. Jack Fish, Warrington coach

"I've never known Warrington to be without a good pack."

In July 1927, almost out of the blue, the Warrington committee appointed Jack Fish as their first team coach and so began another chapter in his remarkable rugby league career. The first team coach in 1927 was not the all-powerful figure of today because it was the committee who actually picked the team, but Fish was able to make suggestions and recommendations and, of course, was in complete charge of training.

Fish was a firm believer in sprint work and never trained over more than 50 or 60 yards himself. "Quickness off the mark, and a finishing burst of speed are great assets," was his philosophy. Fish was to be assisted by trainers Len Green and Jim 'Shint' Daintith, the former Warrington scrum-half who had played in the 1913 Challenge Cup final against Huddersfield.

Two more of Fish's friends and former team-mates – George Dickenson and Bill Harmer – were put in charge of the 'A' team. Dickenson had played alongside Fish in three Challenge Cup finals – 1901, 1904 and 1905 – while Harmer had collected a winner's medal against Hull Kingston Rovers in 1905. Commanding the respect of the players would not be a problem.

The committee also backed the new regime by signing three top-class Welsh players: centres Jesse Meredith and Les Perkins and scrum-half Dai Davies. Meredith, aged 21, was a strong tackler and received a £320 signing-on fee when moving from Abertillery. Club officials travelled to South Wales to watch Newport play Abertillery and signed him immediately after the match.

Perkins, aged 22, was plucked from Cross Keys one week later for a signing-on fee of £475 and was a more creative player. He had twice been a reserve for the Wales rugby union team the previous season, including for their match at Twickenham. Davies was the most costly signing of the lot as Warrington had to pay Broughton Rangers a club record £650 and hand over £250 to the player himself.

New training methods and new signings, of course, seldom deliver instant results and Warrington's league campaign was a huge disappointment as the Wirepullers could only finish 17th in the table with more defeats than victories. The Challenge Cup, however, Jack Fish's favourite competition, was a different matter altogether.

Warrington were drawn away to Kinsley, a mining village near Pontefract, in the first round, but the amateurs accepted £150 to play the tie at Wilderspool. Warrington chose an all-Welsh threequarter line

Jack Fish (second right) in his time as Warrington coach with Len Green, Jim Daintith, Bill Harmer and George Dickenson.

– Billy Rhodes, Jesse Meredith, Les Perkins and Tommy Flynn – who between them scored seven of Warrington's 11 tries in a 43–2 win.

Victories away to Hull Kingston Rovers and at home to Huddersfield followed before Warrington were paired with high-flying Leeds in the semi-final at the Athletic Ground, Rochdale. A crowd of 22,000 assembled to see if Jack Fish's men could pull off a shock and reach the final.

The only try came in the second half when Billy Kirk, the Warrington scrum-half, capitalised on a mistake by Jim Brough, the Leeds full-back and captain. Kirk snapped up the loose ball, raced clear and went over behind the posts. Billy Rhodes kicked the goal and two penalty goals to give Warrington a 9–2 win and earn Jack Fish a fifth Challenge Cup final appearance, albeit as a coach rather than a player.

The final, the last before the move to Wembley in 1929, was against Swinton at Central Park on Saturday, 14 April, and attracted a crowd of almost 34,000. Warrington were again the underdogs and fell behind to an unconverted try from winger Chris Brockbank.

Then, early in the second half, disaster struck when Billy Kirk was severely concussed and play was held up for five minutes while he was treated and eventually carried off on a stretcher. Warrington were reduced to 12 men and a rumour even started that their injured scrum-half was, in fact, dead.

Jack Fish switched Dai Davies, who had been playing on the left wing, to cover for Kirk and moved loose-forward Charlie Seeling to the vacant spot on the wing. Incredibly, Seeling then scored a try in the corner to level matters at 3–3 and fuel hopes of a remarkable Warrington victory.

It was not to be, although the manner of Warrington's 5–3 defeat would remain a source of bitterness for decades to come. Brockbank, who would later become the Warrington secretary, hoisted a huge kick up field towards Arthur Frowen, the Warrington full-back, who had been kicking and tackling immaculately and was their best player.

The wind carried the ball over Frowen's head and he touched it down behind his own try line. The referee, however, ruled that Frowen had first touched the ball in the field of play and awarded a five-yard scrum, with Swinton's head and feed. Swinton won possession and fed the ball to centre Jack Evans who kicked a drop-goal to win the cup. It was a heart-breaking way for the 12 men of Warrington to be denied.

Swinton went on to win all four cups – the Lancashire Cup, the Lancashire League, the Challenge Cup and Championship – becoming the last team to do so, while Warrington finished the season empty handed. It turned out to be Jack Fish's only season in charge because during the summer of 1928 he stood down on health grounds to be replaced by Jim Heesom, the former Warrington forward who had earlier trained him into tip-top condition for the winner-takes-all sprint challenge against Peter 'Bucky' Green.

Fish remained a Warrington supporter and a familiar figure around town and after Warrington reached the Challenge Cup final again in 1933, against Huddersfield, and 1936, against Leeds, and he was asked to explain the club's success in the game's glamour competition.

"I've never known Warrington to be without a good pack," he told the Warrington programme. "We've always had the forwards and that is why we've always done well in cup football. You must have the ball to play this game, and if you have the ball you're keeping it away from the other fellows and that's three parts of the battle.

"And at Warrington we've always had a pack that's been able to get the ball. I don't know what the secret of Warrington's forward power is, but I've a good idea that it's got something to do with the fact that sweeping changes rarely are made in the pack.

"There's nothing more disheartening to a set of backs than to be constantly chasing the other side with the ball. You can go on chasing for a bit, but you get tired of it in the end. You're bound to do.

"When I joined Warrington in 1898 as a lad of 19, the pack was there, and nowadays in 1936, the pack is still there, able and ready to do its job."

During the 1936 cup run, Fish also featured in a rather unflattering cartoon in the *Liverpool Evening Express*, courtesy of the newspaper's resident cartoonist, Bert Wright. He suggested that because Warrington had so many injuries ahead of their semi-final against Salford he had expected to see Fish and the Warrington-born jockey Steve Donoghue in their team.

The 1936 cartoon after Warrington had reached the Challenge Cup Final, showing Jack Fish carrying the jockey Steve Donoghue.

Fish hit the headlines again in December 1938 when the *Warrington Examiner* published his life story in three weekly parts in the build up to his 60th birthday. Part one was headlined "JACK FISH – WIZARD OF RL WING THREEQUARTERS" and the newspaper also carried a page one interview with Bob Anderton, the Warrington club secretary, who said he had "no hesitation in saying that Fish was the finest wing threequarter I have ever seen." Yet again, he was the talk of the town.

With his health fading fast, Fish was admitted to Warrington Borough General Hospital in October 1940. At first, he seemed to improve but he passed away on the morning of Wednesday 23 October – aged 61. The cause of death was given as "chronic myocarditis" which, in layman's terms, is chronic heart disease.

His funeral was held at Warrington Cemetery the following Saturday when Warrington supporters lined the streets as the cortege passed to pay their silent tribute to a great player and entertainer. At the cemetery, eight former Warrington players helped to carry Fish's coffin:

George Dickenson, Jim Daintith, Frank Shugars, Elliot Harris, Tom Hockenhull, Harry Foster, Bert Bradshaw and Joe Lawless. Like Fish, Dickenson and Harris had been members of the 'Aristocratic Four'. The fourth member of the quartet, Danny Isherwood, was also at the graveside. The funeral service was reported in the *Warrington Examiner* as follows:

Funeral of Mr "Jack" Fish
Old Footballers at Graveside

"Old players who had shared in his great triumphs on the playing field, as well as officials and members of Warrington Rugby League Club, and many admirers of his rare abilities as a player, attended the funeral at Warrington Cemetery on Saturday of Mr "Jack" Fish, of 10 York Street, former Warrington, county, and international wing three-quarter, who died in hospital the previous Wednesday morning, as reported in "The Examiner" last week.

In addition to the large and representative gathering at the Cemetery, many townspeople lined the streets as the cortege passed, to pay their tribute to a great player.

The Rev J.E.N. Coleman, curate in charge of St James' Church, Latchford, officiated, and the chief mourners were: Mrs F. Fish, widow; Miss Alice Fish, daughter; Mr John Fish, son; Mrs Ethel Fish, daughter-in-law; Mr and Mrs John Allmark, brother-in-law and sister; Mrs Agnes Hunt and Mrs Edith Jackson, sisters; Mr and Mrs Edward Fish, brother and sister-in-law; Miss Eileen Jackson, niece; Mr and Mrs F Quarmby, brother-in-law and sister-in-law; Mesdames E. Mather, M. Willis, H. Blears and Jessie Barton and Miss Ada Quarmby, sister-in-law; Messrs H. Fish and Sam Fish, cousins.

The following acted as bearers: Messrs G. Dickenson, J. Daintith, F. Shugars, Elliot Harris, T. Hockenhull, Harry Foster, Bert Bradshaw and J. Lawless, old Warrington footballers, and Stan Mann and John Cliffe.

Warrington Rugby League Football Club was represented by the following: Dr James Bennett and Mr E Gibson, trustees, Alderman J.T. Cooper, Captain J. Bainbridge and Mr D. Harold Ward, vice-presidents; and Messrs P.F. Ward, C.L. Ashton, J.W. Gibbs, Edwin Gibson, S. Hayes, J.H. Knowles, E. Lunt, R.F. Anderton, hon. secretary, and S. Jones, hon. treasurer, members of the committee of management. Messrs J. Craik and R. Appleton were unable to attend owing to business reasons.

Old players of the club who attended in addition to the bearers were: Messrs J. Boyle, W. Nevins, I. Hackett, D. Isherwood, E. Jordan, W. Faulkes, T. Kenyon, J. Fairhurst, W. Randells, A. Naylor, W. Harrop, G. Jolley and J. Roach. Others in attendance included Mr F. Bewsick, the former Swinton player, and Mr J. Heesom, the former Warrington Rugby League Club trainer.

Also present were Captain W.C. Field, Messrs T. Williamson, representing Warrington Intermediate Rugby League, T.L. Compton, G. Duckworth, former member of Warrington Rugby Club Committee, P. Barrett, W. Knight, H.W. Lea, T. Mason, J. Cooper, T. Palin, J. Burrows, W. Fairhurst, A. Ashton, W.H. Phillips, former member of Warrington Club committee and secretary of Warrington Billiards League, J. Leslie, S. Hayes, secretary of Warrington Conservative Club, A. Monks, H.T. Williams, former superintendent of the local Corps of the St John Ambulance Brigade, J.L. Stott, J. Shaw, A. Ford, J. Clarke, F. Tomlinson, T.S. Pemberton, H. Gleave, A. Mellor, T. Cannington, W. Hands, J. Ashton, W.I. Gallop, F. Cowsill, Ball and Fogg.

Floral tributes were received from: Wife and Daughter Alice; John, Ethel and baby; Ted Fish and family; Sam and Dorie; Liza, Jack and family; Agnes and family; Edith and family; Jessie and Joe; Sam and Susie (Runcorn); Mrs A Mather and family; Mrs Willis and family; Hannah, Joe and family; Ada; Tom, Lizzie and family; old pal, Stan; Jack, Gertie and boys; a few friends from the Britannia; Molly Skelhorn and mother; Mr and Mrs Heesom (Ring o' Bells); old pal, J Daintith; Mrs Freeman, Freddie and John (Bulls Head); Hilda, Harold, Angela and Sarah (Crown and Sceptre); Mr and Mrs Gibson (Blackburne Arms); Mr Joe Lawless; Mr and Mrs Rigby; Sis and Blanche Mather; friends from the Golden Lion; Mr and Mrs Lowe; Mr and Mrs Rudd and Doreen; Mr and Mrs W. Rudd; Mr and Mrs Lockett; Mrs Cleaton; Tommy Kenyon; Harold and Nellie; old pal Elliot; old pal G. Dickenson; Mr and Mrs R.F. Anderton (White Hart); Mr and Mrs Bert Bradshaw; Charlie Roberts (Farmer's Arms); Warrington Football Club; Warrington Conservative Club; Halifax Rugby Football Club; Mr and Mrs Hockenhull; John and Albert.

Messrs Tom Maguire and Son, of Barbauld Street, had charge of the funeral arrangements."

Two minutes' silence was impeccably observed before Warrington's War Emergency League (Lancashire Section) match against Leigh at Wilderspool that afternoon. Fittingly, Warrington won 23–0 with centre and captain Billy Belshaw scoring a hat-trick of tries.

Fish passed his love of rugby to his son, John, who played at either centre or stand-off for Barnes in the Warrington Junior League in the Thirties and even had trials with Warrington's 'A' team. He also played for Lancashire County Amateurs. After the war, he signed for Salford in August 1946 and played four games for them at right centre without scoring any tries.

John (Jack) Fish junior (right) as coach of Bewsey Towers RFC.

Coincidentally, Fish made his debut against Warrington, at The Willows on 7 September, 1946 – almost 48 years after his father had made his debut for Warrington.

Salford won that game, a Lancashire Cup first round first leg tie, 10–3 in front of 13,000 fans and Fish kept his place in the team for the return leg at Wilderspool seven days later.

For that game, Warrington included a new signing, a 22-year-old Australian winger by the name of Brian Bevan, a man who would go on to smash all of Jack Fish's try-scoring records. Bevan, indeed, scored the first of his 740 tries for Warrington and kicked a goal as the Wire won 10–5, but still went out of the competition 15–13 on aggregate.

John Fish made two more appearances for Salford, both in league games, at Leigh on 2 November and at Bradford on 18 January 1947 before his career fizzled out and he began coaching the Bewsey Towers amateur team.

Brian Bevan, meanwhile, kept on running in the tries and, against Belle Vue Rangers at Wilderspool in November 1950, he overtook Fish's record of 214 tries for the club – a feat no other Warrington player has managed.

The emergence of Brian Bevan inevitably led to comparisons between him and Jack Fish. Will Randles, who played for Warrington in the late 1880s and early 1890s and then trained the team for seven years, thought that Bevan was faster, but that Fish was more elusive.

93

Interviewed in April 1949, he said: "I can still almost picture Jackie tearing away down the touchline towards an opponent, and then stopping dead a yard away. Off he would go again leaving the player looking amazed and very foolish. Bevan does beat opponents but not quite so sensationally as Jackie."

Randles also recalled the winning and losing pay from his playing days. Winning pay was two tuppenny vouchers worth two gills of ale. Losing pay was one tuppenny voucher for just one gill of ale.

Writing in the *Rugby League Gazette* in September 1950, G.A. Brooking sang the praises of both Fish and Bevan: "There is much discussion on the respective merits of Brian Bevan and the late Jack Fish. I have seen both these exponents at their best and my opinion is without prejudice in any way. Brian now appearing on the right and Jack was on the left. Each of them was or is great.

"Jack had plenty of speed with swerve and could dash off the mark almost as quick as lightning slips down an iceberg, as the schoolboy would say. I can never forget one try which Jack Fish made – it was for Lancashire against Yorkshire at Oldham in 1904. Stealing a pass in his own 25 he was off like the wind, with the whole of the visiting team minus the full-back tearing after him like hungry wolves baulked off their prey.

"Facing Gomer Gunn, he swerved past him like the genius he was, and plonked the ball over the line – and the crowd rose to him. Candidly, there is little to choose between Brian and Jack, but I think Jack could do more in confined space than Brian."

Fish was in the news again in October 1952 when the Warrington match day programme ran a "best-ever Warrington team" competition. Brian Bevan topped the poll, but Fish was a close second and the winning selection was: Ben Jolley, Brian Bevan, Bill Shankland, Billy Dingsdale, Jack Fish, Tommy Flynn, Dai Davies, Billy Cunliffe, Dave Cotton, Jack Miller, Jack Arkwright, Harry Bath, Charlie Seeling.

Fish's selection was another source of pride for his widow, Fanny, who was still going strong and would live to the ripe old age of 89, before dying in Warrington in late 1968 – 28 years after the death of her husband.

In 1979, when Bill Garvin, a former Warrington director, wrote a history of the club to mark its centenary, two players were featured on the front cover: Jack Fish and Brian Bevan. Inside, he explained: "Jack Fish and Brian Bevan became legends in their playing days. Both were idolised by Warrington supporters. Fish and Bevan scored many spectacular tries when one was needed to win a match."

The Jack Fish story took another, more unexpected, twist in 1984 with the publication of an article in the *Warrington Messenger* newspaper, claiming that the great Warrington winger had, in fact, become a ghost.

Written by local charity fund-raiser Wally Barnes as part of his "Ghosts of Warrington" series, the story was headlined: "The little runner of the rabbit run or the ghost of Jackie Fish" and went as follows: "In 1940, two army huts were built near the iron bridge over the Manchester Ship Canal at Arpley to house soldiers guarding the very vital bridge of the London Scottish line. What was known as the rabbit run stretched from the iron bridge to the beginning of the old Quay Canal.

"One night in the winter of 1940 during a bombing raid a soldier on guard saw a little plump man running towards him along the rabbit run. The soldier shouted 'halt, who goes there?' but the plump man ran right through the soldier, carried on and disappeared.

"The frightened soldier then refused to go out on guard duty. Three nights later it happened again. The soldier flipped his lid and was sent on sick leave. The ghost of the little plump runner had been seen on many occasions during the late Thirties and Forties.

"The old timers said it was the ghost of one of Warrington's greatest rugby league players of all-time, Jackie Fish, who spent many, quiet, happy hours training along the rabbit run and played for Warrington from 1899 to 1911.

"Jackie was 5 feet 6 inches tall and stocky and known to walk out of the old Ring o'Bells at the bottleneck at Bridge Foot and be sick on the touchline before a game. This happened before the game with the Australian tourists. The Aussies laughingly said: 'is that the great Jackie Fish?' He soon showed them. He scored 18 points to rock the Aussies.

"The trotting ghost was seen by farmers, railwaymen, canal workers and, on one occasion, a group of Aluminium nightshift workers saw him running along the Mersey.

"I once asked my father who was the greatest, Jackie Fish or Brian Bevan. He replied: 'Their styles differed. They were both great but Jackie Fish was the king of RL.' A final word. The rabbit run is still there. Is Jackie Fish?"

Normal service was resumed in September 1998, when the *Warrington Guardian* produced a Wilderspool Centenary magazine, and Fish was named as the player of the decade for 1898 to 1908, Warrington's first 10 years at their new ground.

In 2003, when the Warrington Wolves Past Players' Association launched its Hall of Fame, Fish was one of the 12 founding members, taking his place alongside Jack Arkwright, Brian Bevan, Jim Challinor, Billy Dingsdale, Eric Fraser, Gerry Helme, Albert Johnson, Jack Miller, Harold Palin, Bill Shankland and Tommy Thompson.

He is also featured in the Gillette Rugby League Heritage Centre at the George Hotel in Huddersfield, which was the brainchild of television commentator Mike 'Stevo' Stephenson and opened in 2005.

One of Fish's great grandsons, Grant Mann, is a keen Warrington supporter himself and was at Wembley in 2010 to see the Wolves thrash Leeds Rhinos 30–6 and lift the trophy that Fish had made his own. Understandably, Grant is proud of his great grandfather's career and achievements, and said: "My gran had all his memorabilia in a couple of tins and boxes and when I was a young child, before I hit my early teens, I used to get all the stuff out, menus from posh functions he had been to, badges and caps and things like that. He was a big drinker and he had a lot of faults, I know that, but I am very proud of him and what he meant to the town."

And Fish's legacy to the club also lives on to this day. With Fish inspiring them from his usual spot on the left wing, the Wirepullers became renowned cup fighters, and that is what they remain. Although Warrington have only been crowned champions three times, in 1948, 1954 and 1955, they have won the Challenge Cup seven times and reached 15 finals.

The members of the Rugby League Record-Keepers' Club did an amazing job in the 1970s and 1980s when they compiled the statistics for Warrington and every other professional club. This, of course, was in the days before home computers and the like.

Research for this book, however, has revealed two matches where they may have made slight errors. The first was Leigh versus Warrington on the opening day of the 1904–05 season when Jack Fish was credited with two tries and Elliot Harris one.

Study of the newspapers of the time has suggested that those figures should be reversed – Fish scored only one try and Harris scored twice – and their career records have been amended accordingly. The author feels sure that neither player would mind.

The second match was Warrington versus St Helens on Easter Monday 1909 when the Wirepullers thrashed the Saints 78–6, scoring 20 tries and kicking nine goals. The Rugby League Record-Keepers' Club credited Welsh forward George Thomas with 33 points from five tries and nine goals. Reports in the *Warrington Guardian* and *St Helens Reporter,* however, describe him kicking only eight goals with Jack Fish landing one as well.

Again, their career records have been amended accordingly and again the author feels sure that neither player would mind. George Thomas's 31 points were still a club record that lasted for more than 90 years until a certain Lee Briers came along.

10. The Aristocratic Four

Jack Fish managed many of his achievements in the game, especially for Warrington, as part of the 'Aristocratic Four' threequarter line.

Danny Isherwood

When Danny Isherwood signed for Warrington in 1895 the Wirepullers had a fine threequarter line of Broady, Barber, Cross and Burton made up of Fred Broady, Fair Barber, G. Cross and Charlie Burton. The Aristocratic Four went on to surpass all their achievements.

The leader of the Four, Jack Fish, made 321 appearances for Warrington and, for more than half of those Isherwood was his centre, including in four Challenge Cup finals.

Isherwood's father had played for Warrington during the club's rugby union days and Danny signed for the Wirepullers from the Stockton Heath club, known as the Heathens. He grew up in Stockton Heath and was educated at the People's College in Arpley Street.

Isherwood made his debut on the right wing at home to Wakefield Trinity on 11 April 1896 and so was well established in the first team by the time Warrington signed Fish in October 1898. He was 5 feet 7 inches tall and weighed 11 stones 1 pound.

Isherwood only played centre to Fish once during his first campaign, 1898–99, but after that he made the job his own for eight seasons and 171 appearances, providing the final pass for many of his tries, before George Dickenson inherited the role.

He was not a spectacular player, but he was the ultimate team man, doing whatever it took to get the ball to Fish. He was also the Warrington captain for four years, from 1901 to 1904, suffering Challenge Cup final defeats at the beginning and end of his reign.

A sign of the respect with which Isherwood was held at the club is the fact that he was the first Warrington player to be granted a benefit match – against Broughton Rangers in January 1908. A crowd of 6,622 turned out to honour him and Isherwood was later presented with £165, about £16,500 in today's money.

Fittingly, Isherwood scored the winning try that afternoon. It was his 45th and final try for the club. He was transferred to Leigh for £60 in December 1908 where he spent two seasons, captaining them in their 1909 Lancashire Cup final defeat against Wigan.

During the First World War, he served with the Royal Engineers before returning to Warrington as a committee member in 1921, a post he held for a number of years. Like Dickenson and Elliot Harris, he attended Fish's funeral in 1940 when the Aristocratic Four were reunited for the last time.

Isherwood, lived in Carlton Street in Stockton Heath and died at his home after a long illness on Tuesday 19 January 1943, aged 65. Shortly before his death he had been informed that one of his two sons was missing in action in World War Two, presumed dead. His funeral was held at Hill Cliffe Burial Ground and preceded by a service in Hill Cliffe Baptist Church. Elliot Harris attended, representing the club.

In his obituary, the *Warrington Guardian* stated: "The combination of Jack Fish, Dan Isherwood, George Dickenson and Elliot Harris was the personification of everything that was good in rugby league."

Season	A	T	G	P					
1895–96	2	0	0	0	1905–06	21	2	0	6
1896–97	11	1	0	3	1906–07	26	8	0	24
1897–98	26	2	1	8	1907–08	16	5	0	15
1898–99	26	1	3	9	1908–09	1	0	0	0
1899–00	25	4	0	12	**Totals**	**297**	**45**	**18**	**171**
1900–01	31	6	7	32					
1901–02	19	2	3	12	With Leigh:				
1902–03	22	2	3	12	1908–09	14	2	0	6
1903–04	36	8	0	24	1909–10	23	7	1	23
1904–05	35	4	1	14	**Totals**	**334**	**54**	**19**	**200**

George Dickenson

Warrington centre George Dickenson is sometimes described as the 'odd-man out' in the Aristocratic Four for the simple reason that if his surname had been, say, Simpson, then Fish, Isherwood, Dickenson and Harris would have become Fish, Isherwood, Simpson and Harris and spelt out FISH. As it was, that unusual occurrence only happened twice in 1900 when Welshman Llandaff Smith filled the right centre berth.

In every other respect, however, Dickenson was far from being the 'odd-man out; and played for Lancashire, England and the Northern Union – the team known later as Great Britain – and lined up in the first Anglo-Australian international match at Park Royal, London, on 12 December 1908. The match ended in a 22–22 draw.

Dickenson was the last member of the Aristocratic Four to join the club when he signed, aged 19, at the start of the 1900–01 season. He made his debut at Runcorn that October. He was 5 feet 9 inches tall and weighed 11 stone 2 pounds and a poem of the time perfectly describes his style of play – "Geo Dicky is very tricky, very light and tall" – and he certainly scored his fair share of tries.

He played in three Challenge Cup finals, in 1901, 1904 and 1905, and his leadership skills were recognised when he was appointed Warrington captain for two seasons, 1908–09 and 1909–10.

98

His outstanding service to the club was recognised when he was awarded a testimonial match against St Helens at Wilderspool on Saturday 4 October 1913. Dickenson was made captain for the day and walked out onto the field wearing his county cap, which only arrived just before the match started. The fixture attracted a bumper crowd of 10,008 and made a profit of £271 16s 7d, about £27,000 today. Both figures were slightly higher than even Fish managed to achieve. All the Warrington players paid to watch the match, even though they were playing, and won 22–11 with tries from Bert Bradshaw, Syd Nicholas, Harry Cox and Bert Renwick and five goals from full-back Ben Jolley.

During the First World War, Dickenson served with the Royal Garrison Artillery and that training came in useful when he and Bill Harmer were put in charge of the 'A' team in the summer of 1927, when Fish was named as Warrington coach.

Dickenson, who lived in Winwick Road in Warrington, and Fish became lifelong friends and Dickenson was one of the pall bearers at Fish's funeral in 1940, having sent a floral tribute from "old pal G. Dickenson". He died, aged 71, in June 1953 in the same week as Frank Shugars, who was aged 77, another member of the Challenge Cup-winning team of 1905. Dickenson was buried in Warrington Cemetery while Shugars, who lived in Knutsford Road in Grappenhall, was laid to rest in Grappenhall.

Season	A	T	G	Pts					
1900–01	21	7	0	21	1907–08	35	15	0	45
1901–02	32	6	0	18	1908–09	32	12	3	42
1902–03	26	5	2	19	1909–10	31	10	2	34
1903–04	34	9	6	39	1910–11	32	6	0	18
1904–05	26	4	0	12	1911–12	29	5	0	15
1905–06	16	1	0	3	1912–13	11	0	0	0
1906–07	25	13	0	39	1913–14	25	1	1	5
					Totals	**375**	**94**	**14**	**310**

Elliot Harris

Warrington winger Elliot Harris was the Mark Forster of his day – a local boy made good who simply loved to play rugby. He signed for the Wirepullers from Latchford Rangers in November 1898, one month after Jack Fish had joined from Lostock Gralam. Both were 19 years old and would become team mates for the next eight years.

Ultimately, of course, Harris was overshadowed by the man on the left wing, but was still a fine enough player in his own right to represent Lancashire and appear in the Challenge Cup finals of 1901 and 1904.

Both men were 5 feet 7 inches tall, although at the start of their careers at least, Harris was the heavier man, weighing in at 12 stones 8 pounds, one stone more than Fish. Harris was not quite as quick as Fish, but he was more aggressive and also found time to box in various South West Lancashire towns.

Harris was sent off twice in his career, at Altrincham in a friendly in December 1900 and at Widnes five years later. The latter dismissal was for fighting and earned him a four-week suspension.

Like all rugby players, Harris picked up his fair share of injuries and was particularly unlucky in the 1903–04 campaign when he twice broke his collarbone, first in a pre-season practice match in August and then at Bradford in November.

After the second break, however, he remarked that at least he would be fit for the Challenge Cup and he played in every round as Warrington made it all the way to the final, only to lose to Halifax and earn a second runners-up medal.

Harris's finest individual scoring effort came on Christmas Eve 1898 when he scored a hat-trick of tries at Wilderspool in a friendly match against Birkenhead Wanderers.

Harris loved to play rugby, so much so that when he had stopped playing professionally, he asked to be reinstated as an amateur so that he could continue his career with Cadishead. In November 1909, aged 29, he played for the amateurs against Warrington's 'A' team at Wilderspool on the day that Jim Stuntz made his first appearance in primrose and blue and gave the Australian a torrid time. Harris put in some "vigorous" tackles and the Australian retired injured at half-time.

He passed this love of the game on to his son, Elliot junior, who signed for Warrington in December 1921 and made a number of appearances for the 'A' team.

Harris made headlines again in 1929 when he received the Liverpool Shipwreck and Humane Society Medal for rescuing a woman in the Manchester Ship Canal near Latchford Locks, where he was employed for a number of years, latterly as a bridgeman.

Harris lived at Gate Cottage, Bradshaw Lane, Grappenhall and, from the age of 40, billiards and bowls took up most of his leisure time, but from the age of 60 his interests turned towards animals, especially his ponies and dogs.

Harris and Fish became lifelong friends and Harris was a pall bearer at Fish's funeral, having sent a floral tribute from "old pal Elliot". Harris died in St Helens General Hospital, aged 76, on Christmas Eve 1956. He was buried at Grappenhall Parish Church.

He was the last link with the Aristocratic Four and the glory days of Fish, Isherwood, Dickenson and Harris in the early years of the twentieth century. In another bizarre twist, the four men had died in the order they played: Fish (1940, aged 61), Isherwood (1943, aged 65), Dickenson (1953, aged 71) and Harris (1956, aged 76).

Season	A	T	G	Pts
1898–99	16	4	0	12
1899–00	10	5	0	15
1900–01	19	7	1	23
1901–02	35	13	0	39
1902–03	31	8	0	24
1903–04	23	9	0	27
1904–05	16	6	0	18
1905–06	21	6	0	18
1906–07	1	2	0	6
Totals	**172**	**60**	**1**	**182**

WARRINGTON'S DASHING RIGHT-WINGER.

ELLIOT HARRIS.

(Photo by Mrs. J. Hirst, Warrington.)

Elliot Harris (Courtesy Robert Gate)

Left: Danny Isherwood. Right: George Dickenson

11. Myths and legends

In the years following Jack Fish's retirement as a player, stories about his achievements, records and lifestyle were told, embellished and retold until sometimes it became impossible to separate fact and fable, milestone and myth.

An article in *The Rugby League News*, published in Australia in July 1922, sums this up perfectly. "The story goes that Fish was a wonderful player, both in defence and attack, and as he was such a hard man to train, and was also a great lover of his bitter beer, the crowd would point to him with pride and say 'what would yon lad do if he was sober?'" Newspapers published during Fish's career contain no such claims.

The same issue of *The Rugby League News* also carried a story from the great Australian winger Dan Frawley, who played with Fish for Warrington and against him for the Kangaroos. According to the story, Frawley tried to interest Fish in some cross-country running to build up his fitness and stamina: "After going 100 yards or so he would pull up with a grunt, saying 'I've done enough of this'. Close to the house of the secretary of the club, but out of sight of the house, was a pond, where Jackie would pull up and splash a quantity of the dirty water over his head and face. Then, simulating great distress at his exertions, he would put the word on the secretary for beer money, which was generally forthcoming."

Again, this may be true, it may be false. It may have happened once or it may just be the sort of tale guaranteed to raise a smile at a rugby dinner.

The late Arthur Griffiths has another story about Fish's alleged drinking habits in his book *Memories of an Atherton Pitman*, published in 1990. He writes: "Jackie, in many people's opinion, was one of the greatest three-quarter backs ever to have played professional rugby. He was a very difficult man to hold in a tackle and was as slippery and elusive as an eel, but unfortunately, he had one great failing, to use an old Lancastrian expression, 'he liked his ale', so much so that on Friday evenings prior to a Saturday's match, all the Warrington police, who were enthusiastic supporters of the Warrington team, kept an eye open for Jackie.

"They, the police, knew all Jackie's usual haunts and if they saw that he was getting too drunk, they promptly arrested him on some 'cock and bull' charge and took him to a cell in the town's lock-up. There was a nice comfortable bed in this cell, and he was released the following day in time for the match but not before he had been provided with a good breakfast and if it was a home match, with a good dinner.

"However, on one occasion at least, when Warrington were due to play Leigh at the Mather Lane ground, Jackie managed to elude the vigilant eye of the trainer and got into an ale house at the top of Mather Lane, where he managed to sink quite a number of pints of ale, before being hauled out and persuaded to get into his football kit. He duly lined up with his team at the kick-off, but after being heavily tackled for the first time, he went to the sidelines and was very sick, bringing up a large quantity of ale as well as his dinner. He then returned to the field, recovering very quickly, and went on to play a magnificent game.

"When the 1914 war broke out, Jackie was in the first heavy rush of volunteers and joined the eighth South Lancashires and was sent to Tidworth Pennings on Salisbury Plain, but, alas, Jackie was in rather poor shape and was said to have 'drank' one lung away. He was not discharged but was kept on as a games instructor and, of course, he never went overseas."

Again, there is absolutely no documentary evidence to support the claims that Fish was routinely arrested by the police. So it seems that this story, like so many about the mercurial winger, should be treated with a great deal of suspicion and, as we have seen, Fish's career was sensational enough, without the need for further dramatisation.

Appendices

1. Statistics and records

Warrington

Season	A	T	G	Pts
1898-99	15	8	0	24
1899-1900	21	16	14	76
1900-01	29	22	26	118
1901-02	28	16	23	94
1902-03	26	9	14	55
1903-04	36	16	29	106
1904-05	33	14	25	92
1905-06	16	7	15	51
1906-07	24	24	38	148
1907-08	26	25	13	101
1908-09	33	26	44	166
1909-10	29	28	22	128
1910-11	5	3	0	9
Total	**321**	**214**	**263**	**1,168**

Fish once scored a then club record five tries in a match, against Goole at Wilderspool in the Challenge Cup second round on Saturday 24 March 1900.

He scored four tries in a match on three occasions, against Huddersfield on 20 October 1906, against Swinton on 18 January 1908 and against Merthyr Tydfil on 13 November 1909.

He scored eight hat-tricks and two tries in a match on 33 occasions.

He scored one try or more in 152 matches and his record of 214 tries in 321 appearances gives him a strike rate of one try every one and half games.

He once kicked a then club record nine goals in a match, against Huddersfield at Wilderspool on Saturday 20 October 1906.

He once kicked eight goals in a match, at Merthyr Tydfil on Saturday 10 October 1908.

He also once kicked seven goals in a match, against Goole at Wilderspool in the Challenge Cup second round on Saturday 24 March 1900.

Fish once scored a then club record 30 points in a match, against Huddersfield, as above on 20 October 1906. He also once scored a then Northern Union record 29 points in a match, against Goole at Wilderspool, as above on 24 March 1900.

Players who have scored more than 100 tries for Warrington

Player	Career	Tries
Brian Bevan	1945 to 1962	740
Jack Fish	1898 to1911	214
John Bevan	1973 to 1986	201
Mark Forster	1983 to 2000	191
Parry Gordon	1963 to 1981	167
Albert Naughton	1949 to 1961	167
Billy Dingsdale	1928 to 1940	154
Lee Briers	1997 to 2011	144*
Bobby Greenough	1957 to 1966	136
Jim Challinor	1952 to 1963	135
Brian Glover	1957 to 1970	130
Jim Tranter	1911 to 1928	120
Bob Eccles	1977 to 1987	119
Tommy Thompson	1927 to 1934	112
Albert Johnson	1939 to 1951	112
Gerry Helme	1945 to 1957	101
Lee Penny	1992 to 2003	100

*still playing at the time of writing

Players who have scored more than 1,000 points for Warrington

Player	Career	Points
Lee Briers	1997 to 2011	2,466*
Steve Hesford	1975 to 1985	2,416
Brian Bevan	1945 to 1962	2,288
Harry Bath	1948 to 1957	1,894
Billy Holding	1928 to 1940	1,686
Derek Whitehead	1969 to 1979	1,516
Jack Fish	1898 to 1911	1,168
Laurie Gilfedder	1951 to 1963	1,140
Eric Fraser	1951 to 1964	1,096

*still playing at the time of writing

Players who have kicked more than 200 goals for Warrington

Player	Career	Goals (including drop goals)
Steve Hesford	1975 to 1985	1,159
Lee Briers	1997 to 2011	979*
Billy Holding	1928 to 1940	834
Harry Bath	1948 to 1957	812
Derek Whitehead	1969 to 1979	734
Eric Fraser	1951 to 1964	473
Harold Palin	1936 to 1951	439
Laurie Gilfedder	1951 to 1963	426
Jeff Bootle	1964 to 1969	345
Ben Jolley	1912 to 1926	325
Jack Fish	**1898 to 1911**	**263**
John Woods	1987 to 1989	259
Jonathan Davies	1993 to 1995	258
Paul Bishop	1984 to 1990	225
Chris Bridge	2005 to 2011	210*

*still playing at the time of writing

Jack Fish's tries per competition

League games	161	Friendlies	13
Challenge Cup	36	Lancashire	16
Lancashire Cup	8	England	3
SW Lancs Cup	6	Lancashire trial games	8
Tour games	3	Total	254

Jack Fish's first professional try came against Barrow in a friendly match at Wilderspool on 15 October 1898. His last professional try was in a Challenge Cup first round tie at Coventry on 18 February 1911. He also scored tries in pre-season trial games for Warrington and for Warrington's 'A' team that are not included in this list.

Jack Fish's tries against different clubs and touring sides

Opponents	Apps	Tries
Australia	2	2
Barrow	8	12
Batley	9	3
Bradford	14	8
Brighouse	2	0
Broughton	23	7
Castleford	1	3
Coventry	1	1
Dewsbury	1	0
Ebbw Vale	4	1
Goole	1	5
Halifax	11	2
Heckmondwike	1	3
Huddersfield	7	8
Hull	14	11
Hull KR	5	3
Hunslet	8	4
Keighley	3	1
Leeds	8	5
Leeds Parish Church	1	1
Leigh	22	14
Liverpool	1	3
Merthyr Tydfil	3	7
Morecambe	2	0
Millom	2	0
New Zealand	1	1
Oldham	20	8
Pontefract	1	1
Rochdale Hornets	12	9
Runcorn	22	11
St Helens	22	24
Salford	18	6
Stockport	3	3
Swinton	19	15
Tyldesley	2	2
Wakefield	6	3
Widnes	18	12
Wigan	22	13
Wigan Highfield	1	2
Total	**321**	**214**

Jack Fish's centres

Danny Isherwood	171	Charlie Wood	3
George Dickenson	82	H Berry	2
Tom Hockenhull	12	DH Edmunds	2
Ernie Brookes	8	Llandaff Smith	2
John Cartwright	7	J Ashurst	1
Evan Thomas Jones	6	Harry Forster	1
Jack Duckworth	5	Jack Hallam	1
Ernie Jordan	4	Will McIntyre	1
Ike Taylor	4	D Mahoney	1
G Cross	3	Ernie Ratcliffe	1
Holcroft	3	**Total**	**320**

Fish made one appearance as a centre, to winger Ernie Jordan, at Dewsbury on December 16, 1905.

Lancashire 1901 to 1907

	A	T	G	Pts
Cumberland	7	4	3	18
Cheshire	4	4	1	14
Yorkshire	3	2	1	8
Durham*	2	6	7	32
Total	16	16	12	72

*full title was Durham and Northumberland

England 1904 to 1908

	A	T	G	Pts
Other Nationalities	2	1	0	3
Wales	1	2	2	10
Total	3	3	2	13

The teams for Fish's England matches are included in the main text

2. Lancashire County honours

Jack Fish scored 16 tries in 16 appearances for Lancashire and a further eight tries in six Lancashire trial matches.

Lancashire county trial
Probables 19 (5t, 2g) Possibles 11 (3t, 1g)
Wednesday 3 October 1900 at Knowsley Road, St Helens
Probables: D. Smith (Salford), A. Field (Rochdale H – 1t), T. Williams (Salford), S. Williams (Oldham – 3t), J. Fish (Warrington – 1t, 2g), J.R. Lawton (Oldham), F Morgan (Swinton), W Roberts (Leigh),   W Briers (St Helens), G. Frater (Oldham), J. Rhapps (Salford), G. Aspey (Widnes), F. Treweeke (Barrow), C. Pollitt (Swinton).
Possibles: W. Riggs (Rochdale H), J.T. Liversage (St Helens), R. Wilson (Broughton R), R. Messer (Swinton), V. Hampson (Swinton – 2t, 1g). A. Lees (Oldham), D. Davies (Swinton), D.F. Mereweather (Warrington) J. Moffatt (Oldham), E. Vigors (Swinton – 1t), J. Brown (Wigan), A. Boardman (Warrington), G. Thompson (Broughton R), G. Whitehead (Broughton R), F. Hampson (Widnes).
Referee: J.H. Smith (Widnes)
Half-time: 3–6
Attendance: 3,000

County Championship
Cumberland 2 (1g) Lancashire 21 (5t, 3g)
Saturday, 20 October 1900 at Lonsdale Park, Workington
Cumberland: W. Little (Seaton), G. Whitehead (Millom), J. Young (Millom), J.H. Timmoney (Maryport), J. Varty (Aspatria), J. Leck (Millom), P. Marshall (Wath Brow), J.H. Buckett (Millom – 1g), J. Beetham (Millom), G.W. Lamb (Millom), T. Hall (Whitehaven Rec), J. McLaughlin (Whitehaven Rec), G. Steel (Workington), M. Linton (Seaton), D. Wilson (Wath Brow)
Lancashire: D. Smith (Salford), J. Fish (Warrington – 3g), A. Field (Rochdale H), T. Williams (Salford – 1t), S. Williams (Oldham – 3t), A. Lees (Oldham), D. Davies (Swinton), J. Moffatt (Oldham), P. Tunney (Salford), J. Rhapps (Salford), G. Aspey (Widnes), E. Vigors (Swinton), F. Treweeke (Barrow), W. Briers (St Helens – 1t), C. Thompson (Broughton R)
Referee: F. Renton (Hunslet)
Half-time: 2–6
Attendance: 5,000

Fish was dropped for the games against Yorkshire in November and Cheshire in December, both of which Lancashire won to take the County Championship.

Championship table 1900–01

	P	W	D	L	F	A	Pts
Lancashire	3	3	0	0	75	7	6
Yorkshire	3	2	0	1	55	29	4
Cheshire	3	1	0	2	11	73	2
Cumberland	3	0	0	3	10	42	0

County Championship
Lancashire 8 (2t, 1g), Cheshire 8 (2t, 1g)
Saturday, 26 October, 1901 at Wheater's Field, Broughton
Lancashire: D. Smith (Salford), J. Fish (Warrington– 2t),   R. Valentine (Swinton), R. Wilson (Broughton), S. Williams (Oldham), W. James (Broughton R – 1g), J. Lawton (Oldham), J. Ferguson (Oldham), P. Tunney (Salford), F. Treweeke (Barrow), G. Wilkinson (Oldham), G. Ruddick (Broughton R), W. Briers (St Helens), J. Preston (Swinton), J. Roberts (Leigh)
Cheshire: S. Houghton (Runcorn), W. Hodgson (Stockport), J. Butterworth (Runcorn – 1t), T. Warder (Runcorn), W. Robinson (Stockport), J. Jolley (Runcorn), T. Richardson (Runcorn – 1t), S. Walker (Runcorn), W. Lightfoot (Runcorn), J. Langley (Runcorn), W. Woods (Runcorn), H. Farmer (Runcorn – 1g), W. Oram (Stockport), J. Trotter (Stockport), W. Simister (Stockport)
Referee: T.H. Marshall (Bradford)
Half-time: 5–8
Attendance: 10,000

Lancashire 19 (5t, 2g) Cumberland 3 (1t)
Saturday, 11 January 1902 at Cavendish Park, Barrow
Lancashire: R.L. Thomas (Oldham), J. Fish (Warrington), G. Dickenson (Warrington), A. Hogg (Broughton R – 3t), R. Wilson (Broughton R – 1t), W. James (Broughton R – 1t, 2g), S. James (Broughton R), J. Ferguson (Oldham), P. Tunney (Salford), F. Treweeke (Barrow), G. Wilkinson (Oldham), G. Ruddick (Broughton R), J. Harrison (Rochdale H), J. Preston (Swinton), J. Rhapps (Salford).
Cumberland: T. Pattinson (Aspatria), J.W. Mears (Seaton – 1t), J. Fleming (Millom), T. Fletcher (Seaton), W.F. Kitching (Huddersfield), J. Whitehead (Millom), J. Leck (Millom), J. Beetham (Millom), J. Atkinson (Millom), J. Lazonby (Aspatria), A. Mumberson (Aspatria), J. Owen (Seaton), M. Westmoreland (Whitehaven Rec), E. Timmion (Seaton), J. Grimes (Wath Brow).
Referee: F Renton (Hunslet)
Half-time: 11–3
Attendance: 6,000

Yorkshire 13 (3t, 2g) Lancashire 8 (2t, 1g)
Saturday, 15 February 1902 at The Boulevard, Hull
Yorkshire: H. Taylor (Hull), W.P. Davies (Batley – 2g), T.D. Davies (Leeds), W.J. Eagers (Bradford – 1t), L.I. Deere (Huddersfield), G. Grace (Leeds – 1t), G.H. Marsden (Huddersfield – 1t), T. Broadley (Bradford), A. Laidlaw (Bradford), J. Feather (Bradford), C. Crumpton (Leeds), Jack Riley (Halifax), I. Bartle (Halifax), A. Starks (Hull KR), J. Ritson (Hull).
Lancashire: R.L. Thomas (Oldham), J. Fish (Warrington), D. Isherwood (Warrington), R. Wilson (Broughton R – 2t), V. Hampson (Swinton), W. James (Broughton R – 1g), S. James (Broughton R), J. Ferguson (Oldham), P. Tunney (Salford), F. Treweeke (Barrow), G. Heath (Salford), G. Whitehead (Broughton R), G. Wilkinson (Oldham), J. Evans (Swinton), J. Rhapps (Salford).
Referee: J. Bruckshaw (Stockport)
Half-time: 7–3
Attendance: 15,000 (Receipts: £400)

Championship table 1901–02

	P	W	D	L	F	A	Pts
Cheshire	3	2	1	0	35	11	5
Yorkshire	3	2	0	1	32	26	4
Lancashire	3	1	1	1	35	24	3
Cumberland	3	0	0	3	8	49	0

Non-championship county game
Durham & Northumberland 10 (2t, 2g) Lancashire 49 (9t, 11g)
Wednesday 5 February 1902 at Horsley Park, South Shields
Durham & Northumberland: W. Gurr, H.B. Swainstone (1t), J. Deakin,
W. Hector (2g), W.J. Archer (1t), J. Clegg, G. McCann (Wallsend),
R. Thompson, J. Marshall, R. Hindson, T. Sowerby, G. Newman, T. Hamilton
(St Pauls), G. Dickenson (Halifax), E. Rawlings (Wallsend)
Lancashire: R.L. Thomas (Oldham), J. Fish (Warrington – 3t, 3g), T. Bowker
(Barrow), R. Wilson (Broughton R – 1t), V. Hampson (Swinton – 1t), W. James
(Broughton R – 8g), S. James (Broughton R), J. Ferguson (Oldham), P. Tunney
(Salford), F. Treweeke (Barrow), G. Heath (Salford – 1t), G. Whitehead
(Broughton R – 3t), J. Harrison (Rochdale H), J. Evans (Swinton), J Rhapps
(Salford)
Referee: F. Renton (Hunslet)
Half-time: 4–14
Attendance: 2,000

All the Durham & Northumberland players were from the South Shields club
unless otherwise stated.

Fish was presented with his Lancashire county cap in May 1902.

Lancashire county trial
Probables 21 (5t, 3g) Possibles 7 (1t, 2g)
Monday 6 October, 1902 at Lowerhouse Lane, Widnes
Probables: J. Fielding (Broughton R), A. Hogg (Broughton R), R. Wilson
(Broughton R), G. Dickenson (Warrington – 2t), J. Fish (Warrington – 2t, 1g),
W. James (Broughton R – 2g), S. James (Broughton R), P. Tunney (Salford),
J. Rhapps (Salford), G. Heath (Salford), J. Ferguson (Oldham), G Whitehead
(Broughton R), G. Wilkinson (Oldham), J. Evans (Swinton – 1t), A. Boardman
(Warrington)
Possibles: J.H. Tilley (Widnes), B. Wilson (Barrow), T. Bowker (Barrow),
H. Bennett (Leigh), E. Harris (Warrington), J. Lomas (Salford – 1t, 2g),
J.H. Molyneux (Leigh), J. Green (St Helens), J. Carney (St Helens),
G. Boardman (Leigh), J. Roberts (Leigh), G. Frater (Oldham), J. Brown
(Wigan), W. Oram (Broughton R), J. Curtis (Widnes)
Substitute: F. Harry (Broughton R) for Bowker
Referee: J.H. Smith (Widnes)
Half-time: 5–5
Attendance: 1,500

County Championship
Cheshire 3 (1t) Lancashire 11 (3t, 1g)
Saturday, 25 October 1902 at Irwell Lane, Runcorn
Cheshire: S. Houghton (Runcorn), D. Jones (Runcorn), J. Butterworth (Runcorn), T. Warder (Runcorn), W. Hodgson (Stockport – 1t), T. Richardson (Runcorn), W. Booth (Stockport), S. Walker (Runcorn), J. Williams (Runcorn), W. Woods (Runcorn), A. Moulton (Runcorn), H. Farmer (Runcorn), J. Tomlinson (Runcorn), H. Foster (Stockport), J. Brown (Birkenhead W)
Lancashire: D. Smith (Salford), E. Harris (Warrington), R. Wilson (Broughton R – 2t), R. Valentine (Swinton), J. Fish (Warrington), W. James (Broughton R – 1t, 1g), S. James (Broughton R), P. Tunney (Salford), J. Rhapps (Salford), G. Heath (Salford), J. Ferguson (Oldham), G. Frater (Oldham), G. Boardman (Leigh), J. Evans (Swinton), W. Oram (Broughton R).
Referee: W Robinson (Manningham)
Half-time: 8–0
Attendance: 4,000

Lancashire 13 (3t, 2g) Yorkshire 0
Saturday 15 November 1902 at Weaste, Salford
Lancashire: D. Smith (Salford), A. Hogg (Broughton R – 1t), R. Wilson (Broughton R), R. Valentine (Swinton – 1t, 1g), J. Fish (Warrington – 1t), W. James (Broughton R – 1g), S. James (Broughton R), P. Tunney (Salford), J. Rhapps (Salford), G. Heath (Salford), J. Ferguson (Oldham), G. Frater (Oldham), G. Boardman (Leigh), J. Evans (Swinton), W. Oram (Broughton R).
Yorkshire: H. Taylor (Hull), W.P. Davies (Batley), T.D. Davies (Leeds), W.J. Eagers (Bradford), E.W. Bennett (Wakefield T), G.H. Marsden (Bradford), G. Grace (Leeds), T. Broadley (Bradford), A. Starks (Hull KR), I. Bartle (Halifax), Jack Riley (Halifax), A. Laidlaw (Bradford), C. Crumpton (Leeds), P. Driver (Huddersfield), F. Littlewood (Huddersfield).
Referee: J Kidd (Millom)
Half-time: 3–0
Attendance: 14,000 (Receipts: £433)

Cumberland 3 (1t) Lancashire 21 (5t, 3g)
Saturday, 10 January 1903 at Salthouse, Millom
Cumberland: J. Robley (Maryport), B. Wilson (Barrow), J.H. Timmoney (Maryport – 1t), J. Varty (Parton), W. Kitchen (Huddersfield), R. Messenger (Maryport), W. Dixon (Maryport), J.W. Beetham (Broughton R), T. Dixon (Parton), J. Smallwood (Whitehaven Rec), M. Varty (Seaton), E.K. Tinnion (Seaton), J. Benn (Maryport), S. Hoggarth (Millom), H. Templeman (Workington).
Lancashire: D. Smith (Salford), A Hogg (Broughton R – 3t), R. Wilson (Broughton R – 1t), G. Dickenson (Warrington), J. Fish (Warrington – 1t), S. James (Broughton R – 3g), J. Lomas (Salford), P. Tunney (Salford), J. Rhapps (Salford), G. Heath (Salford), A. Boardman (Warrington), J. Ferguson (Oldham), W. Oram (Broughton R), G Boardman (Leigh), J. Evans (Swinton).
Referee: J.M. Sedman (Liversedge)
Half-time: 3–11

Championship table 1902–03

	P	W	D	L	F	A	Pts
Lancashire	4	4	0	0	55	11	8
Yorkshire	4	2	0	2	44	25	4
Cheshire	4	2	0	2	27	24	4
Durham*	4	1	0	3	9	23	2
Cumberland	4	1	0	3	12	64	2

*full name: Durham & Northumberland

Fish was not selected for the match against Durham & Northumberland at Wheater's Field, Broughton, on Wednesday 10 December 1902

Lancashire county trial
Probables 31 (7t, 5g) Possibles 8 (2t, 1g)

Monday 12 October 1903 at Wilderspool, Warrington

Probables: D. Smith (Salford), J .Fish (Warrington – 2t, 3g), R. Wilson (Broughton R – 1t), A. Hogg (Broughton R – 1t), J. Lomas (Salford – 1t, 2g), J. Baxter (Rochdale H), P. Tunney (Salford), J. Rhapps (Salford), G. Heath (Salford – 1t), J. Ferguson (Oldham), G. Frater (Oldham), G. Boardman (Leigh – 1t).

Possibles: R.L. Thomas (Oldham), G. Dickenson (Warrington), P. Thomas (Oldham), J. Leytham (Lancaster), J. Lally (Widnes), J. Molyneux (Leigh), A. Boardman (Warrington), H. Buckler (Salford), F. Lee (St Helens – 1t), J.R. Hilton (Wigan), W. Brown (Salford), G. Aspey (Widnes).

NB: The backs changed sides at half-time and Fish scored a try and a goal for Possibles.

Referee: J.H. Smith (Widnes)
Half-time: 28–0
Attendance: 2,000

County championship
Lancashire 26 (8t, 1g) Cheshire 5 (1t, 1g)

Wednesday 28 October 1903 at Wheater's Field, Broughton

Lancashire: D. Smith (Salford), J. Fish (Warrington – 2t, 1g), R. Wilson (Broughton R – 3t), A. Hogg (Broughton R – 2t), W. James (Broughton R), W. James (Broughton R), J. Baxter (Rochdale H – 1t), P. Tunney (Salford), J. Rhapps (Salford), G. Heath (Salford), J. Ferguson (Oldham), G. Frater (Oldham), G. Boardman (Leigh).

Cheshire: E. Harrison (Runcorn), J. Dutton (Runcorn), J. Butterworth (Runcorn), J.E. Davies (Birkenhead), J. Richardson (Runcorn), J. Molyneux (Leigh – 1g), S. Walker (Runcorn), W. Woods (Runcorn), A. Moulton (Runcorn), A. Richardson (Runcorn), J.W. Davies (Birkenhead – 1t), J. Belton (Birkenhead).

Referee: W Robinson (Manningham)
Half-time: 12–5
Attendance: 3,000 (Receipts: £79)

Durham & Northumberland 0 Lancashire 42 (10t, 6g)
Wednesday 9 December 1903 at Horsley Park, South Shields
Durham & Northumberland: W.H. Gurr (South Shields), F. Mawhood (South Shields), R. Thompson (South Shields), J. Ritson (Hull), E. Ellis (South Shields), McCann (South Shields), J. Bell (Salford), R. Shaw (Salford), G. Newman (South Shields), A. Peat (South Shields), C.W. Cox (South Shields), T. Sowerby (South Shields).
Lancashire: D. Smith (Salford), J. Fish (Warrington – 3t, 4g), R. Wilson (Broughton R – 2t), A. Hogg (Broughton R – 1t), J. Lomas (Salford – 2t, 2g), J. Baxter (Rochdale H), P. Tunney (Salford – 1t), G. Heath (Salford), H. Buckler (Salford), J. Ferguson (Oldham), A. Boardman (Warrington – 1t), G. Boardman (Leigh).
Referee: W Robinson (Manningham)
Half-time: 0–19
Attendance: 1,000

Lancashire 15 (3t, 3g) Cumberland 0
Wednesday 13 January 1904 at Central Park, Wigan
Lancashire: D. Smith (Salford), J. Fish (Warrington – 1t), P. Thomas (Oldham – 1t), A. Hogg (Broughton R – 1t), J. Lomas (Salford – 3g), J. Baxter (Rochdale H), P. Tunney (Salford), J. Rhapps (Salford), H. Buckler (Salford), A Boardman (Warrington), G. Frater (Oldham), G. Boardman (Leigh).
Cumberland: R. Petrie (Seaton), T. Smith (Maryport), J.H. Timmoney (Maryport), W. Crane (Workington), J. Jackson (Hunslet), P.W. Marshall (Parton), T. Jacques (Wath Brow), H. Marland (Maryport), W. Young (Parton), S.W. Pinquey (Workington), J. Labourne (Seaton), J. Nelson (Whitehaven Rec).
Referee: F. Renton (Hunslet)
Half-time: 5–0
Attendance: 4,000 (Receipts: £80)

Championship table 1903–04

	P	W	D	L	F	A	Pts
Lancashire	4	4	0	0	91	5	8
Yorkshire	4	3	0	1	60	29	6
Cheshire	4	2	0	2	30	62	4
Durham	4	1	0	3	29	84	2
Cumberland	4	0	0	0	17	47	0

Lancashire county trial
Probables 15 (3t, 3g) Possibles 17 (3t, 4g)
Wednesday 12 October 1904 at Central Park, Wigan
Probables: J. Hallam (Warrington), C. Creevey (St Helens – 2t), R. Wilson (Broughton R), J. Lomas (Salford – 1t, 3g), J. Fish (Warrington), S. James (Broughton R), W. James (Broughton R), J. Rhapps (Salford), J. Ferguson (Oldham), G. Frater (Oldham), A. Boardman (Warrington), J.R. Hilton (Wigan), G. Thomas (Warrington), D. Thomas (Oldham), J. Preston (Warrington).
Possibles: R.W. Poole (Broughton R), J. Hughes (Widnes – 2t), F. Harry (Broughton R), I. Taylor (Widnes), J. Leytham (Wigan – 1g), W. Anderson (Wigan – 3g), B. Kirk (Leigh), J. Trotter (Broughton R), H. Buckler (Salford), J.H. Wilkinson (Oldham), P. O'Neill (Leigh – 1t), W. Prescott (St Helens),

114

W. Brown (Salford), J. Brown (Wigan), W. Todd (Chadderton).
Referee: J.H. Smith (Widnes)
Half-time: 10–2
Attendance: 5,000

County championship
Cheshire 3 (1t) Lancashire 0
Wednesday 26 October 1904 at Irwell Lane, Runcorn
Cheshire: S. Houghton (Runcorn), J. Dunbavin (Bradford), H. Price (Runcorn), J. Butterworth (Runcorn), S. Johnson (Leigh), J. Richardson (Runcorn – 1t), J.H. Dunbavin (Leigh), S. Walker (Runcorn), J .Tomlinson (Runcorn), A. Richardson (Runcorn), R. Padbury (Runcorn), J. Dixon (Runcorn), T. Cook (Warrington), M. McDonald (Widnes), R. Jones (Birkenhead).
Lancashire: R.W. Poole (Broughton R), J. Fish (Warrington), J. Lomas (Salford), I. Taylor (Widnes), A. Hogg (Broughton R), W. Anderson (Wigan), W. James (Broughton R), G. Thomas (Warrington), J. Ferguson (Oldham), J. Rhapps (Salford), W. Prescott (St Helens), D. Thomas (Oldham), H. Buckler (Salford), J. Trotter (Broughton R), J.H. Wilkinson (Oldham).
Referee: W. Robinson (Manningham)
Half-time: 3–0
Attendance: 3,000

Lancashire 5 (1t, 1g) Yorkshire 14 (4t, 1g)
Saturday 12 November 1904 at Watersheddings, Oldham
Lancashire: R.W. Poole (Broughton R), A. Hogg (Broughton R), I. Taylor (Widnes), F. Harry (Broughton R), J. Fish (Warrington – 1t, 1g),   J. Lomas (Salford), T. Hockenhull (Warrington), J. Preston (Warrington), J. Ferguson (Oldham), P. O'Neill (Leigh), D. Thomas (Oldham), W. Prescott (St Helens), W. Cheetham (Swinton), J. Trotter (Broughton R), H. Buckler (Salford).
Yorkshire: G. Gunn (Bradford), J. Dechan (Bradford), E.P. Mosby (Bradford – 1t, 1g), Joe Riley (Halifax), W.P. Davies (Batley – 2t), G.H. Marsden (Bradford – 1t), T. Surman (Bradford), A. Starks (Hull KR), W. Brooke (Hunslet), W.T. Osborne (Hull KR), A. Laidlaw (Bradford), J. Kilburn (Hull), G.H. Langhorn (Halifax), W. Morton (Halifax), H. Wilson (Halifax).
Referee: J. Bruckshaw (Stockport)
Half-time: 5–0
Attendance: 8,500 (Receipts: £208)

Cumberland 11 (3t, 1g) Lancashire 0
Monday 16 January 1905 at the Recreation Ground, Whitehaven
Cumberland: W.J. Eagers (Bradford), J. Flynn (Swinton), E. Austin (Millom – 1t), T. Fletcher (Seaton), W.R. Wedgewood (Halifax – 2t, 1g),   J. Jackson (Hunslet), J. Marshall (Parton), J. Benn (Broughton R), A. Hutton (Brookland R),   M. Westmoreland (Bradford), C. Marland (Maryport),   T. Banks (Parton), J. Owens (Oldham), J. Ritson (Hull), J. Kelly (Oldham).
Lancashire: R.W. Poole (Broughton R), J. Leytham (Wigan), R. Wilson (Broughton R), F. Harry (Broughton R), J. Fish (Warrington), S. James (Broughton R), T. Hockenhull (Warrington), J. Ferguson (Oldham), J. Trotter (Broughton R), P. O'Neill (Leigh), J. Preston (Warrington), W. Prescott

(St Helens), H. Buckler (Salford), W. Cheetham (Swinton), D. Thomas (Oldham).
Referee: J.H. Oakland (Barnsley)
Half-time: 3–0
Attendance: 1,500

Championship table 1904–05

	P	W	D	L	F	A	Pts
Yorkshire	3	3	0	0	44	8	6
Cheshire	3	2	0	1	8	14	4
Cumberland	3	1	0	2	16	23	2
Lancashire	3	0	0	3	5	28	0

Lancashire county trial
Probables 31 (7t, 5g) Possibles 15 (3t, 3g)
Wednesday 27 September 1905 at Wheater's Field, Broughton
Probables: R.W. Poole (Broughton R), J. Fish (Warrington – 1t), R. Wilson (Broughton R – 2t), J. Lomas (Salford – 2g), J. Leytham (Wigan – 3t, 1g), S. James (Broughton R – 1g), T. White (Oldham – 1t), A. Boardman (Warrington), G. Thomas (Warrington), J. Preston (Warrington – 1g), P. O'Neill (Leigh), W. Cheetham (Swinton), H. Buckler (Salford), W. Prescott (St Helens), S. Walker (Runcorn).
Possibles: H. Gifford (Barrow), W. Harris (Broughton R – 3g), F. Harry (Broughton R – 1t), J. Butterworth (Runcorn), A. Hogg (Broughton R – 1t), D. Preston (Salford), J. Thomas (Wigan), R. Tyrer (Wigan), T. McCabe (Widnes), M. McDonald (Widnes), A. Lee (Leigh), F. Lee (St Helens), R. Silcock (Leigh – 1t), T. Pomfret (Swinton), W. Morgan (Barrow).
Referee: J.H. Smith (Widnes)
Half-time: 13–10
Attendance: 1,000

County championship
Lancashire 3 (1t) Cumberland 3 (1t)
Saturday 7 October 1905 at Central Park, Wigan
Lancashire: R.W. Poole (Broughton R), J. Leytham (Wigan), J. Lomas (Salford), R. Wilson (Broughton R), J. Fish (Warrington – 1t), S. James (Broughton R), D. Preston (Salford), A. Boardman (Warrington), W. Cheetham (Swinton), R. Silcock (Leigh), P. O'Neill (Leigh), F. Lee (St Helens), D. Rees (Salford), J. Trotter (Broughton R), R. Tyrer (Wigan).
Cumberland: W.B. Little (Halifax), F. Austin (Millom), T. Fletcher (Oldham), W.J. Eagers (Hunslet), J.T. Flynn (Swinton), W. Dixon (Oldham), M. Jenkinson (Wath Brow – 1t), J. Ferguson (Oldham), H. Marland (Hull), J. Kelly (Egremont), W. Winskill (Broughton R), S. Connors (Brookland R), J.L. Clampitt (Millom), G. Pinguey (Workington), J. Owens (Oldham).
Referee: F. Renton (Hunslet)
Half-time: 3–3
Attendance: 12,000
Receipts: £230

Fish was injured in the act of scoring Lancashire's only try.

Lancashire county trial
Probables 11 (3t, 1g) Possibles 17 (5t, 1g)
Monday 30 September 1907 at Wilderspool, Warrington
Probables: H. Gifford (Barrow), J. Leytham (Wigan – 1t, 1g), B. Jenkins (Wigan
– 1t), J. Butterworth (Runcorn), S. Johnson (Leigh – 1t), J. Jolley (Runcorn),
T. White (Oldham), P. O'Neill (Leigh), J. Beetham (Broughton R), D. Rees
(Salford), A. Naylor (Warrington), R. Padbury (Runcorn), A. Smith (Oldham).
Possibles: W. Dixon (Oldham), J. Fish (Warrington – 2t), D. Isherwood
(Warrington – 1g), H. Price (Wigan), G. Tyson (Oldham – 1t), E. Brookes
(Warrington), J. Thomas (Wigan), D. Davies (Swinton), F. Mooney (St Helens),
W. Simister (Swinton), A. Hannah (Barrow), E. Thomas (Salford), J. Spencer
(Salford – 2t).
Referee: W. Nevins (Warrington)
Half-time: 2–8
Attendance: 2,000

County championship
Lancashire 3 (1t) Cumberland 7 (1t, 2g)
Saturday 5 October 1907 at Wheater's Field, Broughton
Lancashire: H. Gifford (Barrow), J. Fish (Warrington – 1t), R. Wilson
(Broughton R), B. Jenkins (Wigan), J. Leytham (Wigan), J. Thomas (Wigan),
J. Jolley (Runcorn), A. Hannah (Barrow), R. Padbury (Runcorn), W. Simister
(Swinton), J. Beetham (Broughton R), J. Spencer (Salford).
Cumberland: W.B. Little (Halifax – 1g), A. Brown (Workington), W. Hillen (St
Helens), W. Dixon (Oldham), W.F. Kitchen (Huddersfield – 1t), J. Lomas
(Salford – 1g), J. Flynn (Broughton R), J. Ferguson (Oldham), J. Owens
(Oldham), W. Winskill (Broughton R), J.L. Clampitt (Broughton R), D. Davies
(Swinton), C. Brown (Barrow), J.W. Trotter (Broughton R).
Referee: R Robinson (Bradford)
Half-time: 3–5
Attendance: 5,000

Appendix 3: Jack Fish interview

The following major newspaper interview with Jack Fish was published on Saturday 5 October 1907 as part of a series entitled "My Football Career: weekly talks with leading players". It was published 11 weeks before Warrington played the New Zealand 'All Golds' at Wilderspool on Saturday 21 December.

We have chosen a big subject for our football sketch this week – "Jack" Fish, of Warrington, otherwise known in some quarters as "the elusive and irrepressible Mr Fish." Just for the time being he is not quite so elusive as we have sometimes known him, for, you see, he is qualifying for an aldermanic chair, and when a man has added a couple of stones to his normal fighting weight, it stands to reason that he is likely to be somewhat retarded in his movements. This question of poundage is one that asserts itself during each close season, but really it causes little or no trouble to Mr Fish.

By the by, there is no obvious reason, beyond the fact that it sounds rather nice and novel, why we should now be referring to him as Mr Fish. Only once has he been known to respond to that appellation. That was when in the only year of his Warrington captaincy he heard the Northern Union officials invite "Mr" Fish to accept the brimming Cup which he and his comrades had so worthily won. No one could have responded with more alacrity. This digression will be pardoned, for it refers to what Fish himself alludes to as "the proudest moment of my life." To return to the question of avoirdupois, we know of no footballer who adds weight so rapidly out of season but who can reduce it so quickly when the season commences. We have heard of him turning the scale at 14st 4lb at the end of August, and being down at 12st 4lb by the end of September. How he manages it, he will narrate hereafter.

Just now, by reason of that excessive weight of which we have spoken, he is not being seen at his best. We saw him on Monday, for the Lancashire "Possibles" against the "Probables," score a brilliant try, daring in its inception and remarkable in its realisation. But it was a spasmodic effort, and in his general play his lack of condition told its tale. The Lancashire Committee are still content to put their trust in him, as they showed by selecting him for today's county match, for they know their man, and they, like all competent authorities, still regard him as the best wing three-quarter in the Northern Union. Personally, the writer has no doubt on this point – that his equal on the wing has not been seen in the North of England this last half-dozen years. Agile as a cat, one of the fastest runners of his day at a fifty yards sprint, and possessed of wonderful dodging powers, he has,

118

during his ten years with Warrington, earned for himself a fame in club and county football that will last for all football time.

Warrington's best investment
We are used to his ways in the North now, but so long as wing three-quarter play remains what it is men will never tire of the masterful tactics of Master Fish. His swerve is at once an education and a fascination. He was the "star" of Warrington when on that first day with them he scored a try against Barrow which made spectators rub their eyes in wonder, and he has remained the "star" of Warrington ever since. What a treasure Fish has been to the Wilderspool organisation! He cost the club no more than a £5 note when he signed the Warrington professional form, and to-day his transfer could not be secured for fifty "fivers," for they know his worth at Wilderspool. He is not yet 28 years old, so he has many years of faithful service still left in him.

Fish is a footballer by heredity. "My father," he told the writer, "was a footballer before me. He played as a forward in the early days of the Runcorn Club, and I have heard men say what a rare forward he was, too. I was born at Runcorn 28 years come this December, so I am a Cheshire man, though I have never chosen to wear the Cheshire colours. My apprenticeship of football was served in Cheshire – at the village of Lostock Gralam, near Northwich. I was in at forming a junior Rugby club there when I was 15 years old, and it was through that club that I got my introduction to Warrington." Exactly how that introduction came about Fish himself only knows from hearsay.

The "discovery" of Fish as an embryo "star" of Northern Union football was left to a Warrington committeeman. It happened that Warrington were in search of talent, and one of their emissaries for the period was that old forward J.T. Thorniley, who saw Fish play with Lostock Gralam. Thorniley came back to Warrington with glowing accounts of the jewel he said he had unearthed. He spoke superlatively of Fish's qualifications, though he was then but a lad, and on the strength of his assurance a match was arranged between Lostock Gralam and the Warrington 'A' team, that the Warrington committee might themselves see how far Thorniley was right in his judgment. Fish rendered a notable account of himself that day, and when he had scored four tries in convincing style the Wilderspool organisation made overtures to him, and signed him on as a Warrington player.

Fish's great scoring achievements
Fish was straightaway drafted into the Warrington first team, and in his first match with them, which was against Barrow, he set the seal upon his success by scoring a magnificent try in the first two minutes of the

game. His career as a first-class footballer dates from that day, and has been marked by an unbroken series of personal triumphs. There are many scoring feats in Fish's career that are entitled to rank as local records, if nothing more. We will let him instance them in his own way. "My best scoring season was seven years ago, when I ran up 176 points in the season's matches. I had two big days in that season. One was when we met Goole in the cup-ties. I scored seven goals and five tries that day (29 points), but that was a record which I just beat last season, when, in the match at Huddersfield, I scored eight goals and five tries (31 points). On another occasion, in a Lancashire county match against Durham at South Shields, I scored 28 points."

Of all the sensational tries scored by Fish, none ranks so high in his own estimation as that which he scored against Oldham in last year's cup final, when he intercepted a pass intended for Tyson, dribbled the length of the field, then picked up and dashed over. There was another occasion – the cup semi-final, between Warrington and Bradford, at Rochdale – when he was the hero of the tale of a stolen pass. Anyone who witnessed the match will not have forgotten how he took the ball as it was being passed between Connell and Mosby, and scored the try which was practically the turning-point of the game. It is singular that some of Fish's best performances have been against Bradford. Another try of his that Bradfordians remember occurred three years ago, when, on the Wilderspool ground, changing his usual tactics, he bored his way through six of the Bradford defenders and scored the winning try.

A much-injured player
Fish's great service to Warrington is indicated by the fact that he has assisted them twice to win the West Lancashire Cup; he has played for them in four Northern Union Cup finals, two of which they have won; and captained them last season when they won the Lancashire Cup against Broughton Rangers at Wigan. The Central Park ground, by the bye, has a peculiar fatality for Fish. In five successive appearances there he has sustained a broken leg, a broken collar-bone, two dislocated ankles, and a broken arm. Despite these injuries, he is by no means a "crock" yet. Warrington people, at any rate, regard him too highly to ever think of letting him go elsewhere, though last season he was only able to assist their club in 14 matches.

Our interviewer asked Fish how he came to make his mark as a three-quarter. He replied: "Well, I suppose it was due to instinct and natural qualities more than anything else. I must say, however, that when I found out that I could run a bit I determined that I would practise a new way of scoring tries. I do not know that I built my style on anybody else's pattern. I did not get the idea of swerving from anybody else, nor did anyone teach me how to do it. It occurred to me that to go bald-headed for the line, and try to force one's way through did not always pay. I determined to cultivate the art of dodging, and in course of practice I cultivated what you call a swerve.

How he learned to swerve

"But it cost me many an hour, and days and weeks of careful practice. This is how I learned to swerve. I used to get a number of sticks, and place them in a row at distances of four or five yards apart. Then I would start off at a run, and wind my way in and out between the sticks without diminishing my pace. Gradually I lessened the distance between the sticks, until finally I was able to run down the row with the sticks only a few feet apart. I can commend that method to anybody who wants to learn to swerve. It certainly served my purpose most effectively. Of course, to be able to swerve effectively you have got to be a bit of a sprinter. I have always fancied myself as a sprinter, and can do a bit even yet.

"It is only two years since I ran 'Bucky' Green at Wigan, for £50 a side, and won. That was when people thought I had gone off my running altogether. I think I should have gone in for running really seriously if the Amateur Athletic Association had not put the ban on Northern Union players, and declared them professionals. Perhaps you will be surprised when I tell you that even that has not stopped me from winning a good few prizes during the last year or two. I have altogether won £123 in prizes for running, besides 14 medals. It was only last year that I brought two prizes from a meeting in the North of England." – There are few places evidently where Fish is unknown. – "There was a time when I could do the hundred yards in just over even time, and even now, with a little bit of training, I can always do it in eleven seconds. I do not say I could do it to-day, with my present weight.

An opinion upon training

"Talking about weight, I reckon there are few men who put on weight as I do. But there are none who can reduce it more quickly. You may be surprised when I tell you that I have scaled as much as 14st 4lb at the end of the close season, and yet a few weeks later I have been able to play football at just over 12st. To-day I am 12st 8lbs, but you can depend upon it I shall be under 12st by the time the New Zealanders come to Warrington. Then we shall see if I can do a bit of swerving.

"If you want to know the secret of reducing weight, it lies in training, and the sort of training I always adopt is this, I go for a course of hot baths, and plenty of walking exercise. There is nothing

AND WE
SIGHED FOR.
THE GOOD OLD DAYS OF FISH & LOMAS,
THAT IS, EXCEPT FISH &' LOMAS, WHO .
SEEMED CONTENT TO BE OUT OF IT. BUT
FISH & CHIPS CONSOLED A LOT OF WIGAN

Jack Fish (left) and Jimmy Lomas were sketched chatting during the 1936 Lancashire Cup final between Salford and Wigan at Wilderspool. Salford won a dreary contest 5-2.
(Courtesy Graham Morris)

like walking for a footballer. It beats skipping into 'a cocked hat.' In fact, I reckon skipping does a man harm, for it weakens the ankles. Indian club exercises are a fine thing, but when all is said, the best training is in walking, and a further wrinkle as to the best place for training is this – go to Blackpool."

Further conversation with Fish elicits from him a warm admiration for his colleague and partner "Dan" Isherwood, to whose intelligent tactics and judgment in passing he attributes much of his own success as a scorer. "But by far the greatest centre I have ever seen," he adds, "is 'Jimmy' Lomas. Never in my best days could I hold a candle to Lomas as an individualist. If you want my opinion on the point, I should say that Lomas is the finest all-round man that the Northern Union has produced."

N.B. Lomas, in return, had great respect for Fish. In his 1930s memoirs featured in the excellent biography *The King of Brilliance* by Graham Morris, published by London League Publications Ltd last year, Lomas wrote: "Jack Fish was the human ferret. I have never seen his like before or since. He could get through the eye of a needle."

4. Injuries

It was sometimes said that Jack Fish was too brave for his own good. Here, apart from the everyday bumps, bruises and strains, are some of the injuries he suffered:

Bruised shoulder: February 1899.
Fractured cartilage in left hand: January 1903.
Damaged thumb: January 1904.
Bruised ribs: October 1904.
Broken nose: December 1904.
Broken shoulder: October 1905.
Broken left leg (tibia): January 1906.
Broken right forearm (two places): December 1906.
Badly sprained ankle: February 1909

5. Family matters

For the 1881 Census, Jack Fish lived at 7 Lowes Court, 98 Cooper Street, Runcorn: Richard Fish, head of house, aged 25, labourer, born Runcorn, Cheshire; Mary A. Fish, wife, aged 22, born Runcorn, Cheshire; John Fish, son, aged 2, born Runcorn, Cheshire.

For the 1891 Census, Jack Fish lived at 57 Cooper Street, Runcorn: Richard Fish, head of house, aged 35, chemical labourer; Mary Ann Fish, wife, aged 33; John Fish, son, aged 12, scholar; Eliza Jane Fish, daughter, aged 8, scholar; Agnes Fish, daughter, aged 5, scholar; Samuel Henry Fish, son, aged 2; Annie Fish, daughter, aged 1. All born in Runcorn, Cheshire.

For the 1901 Census, Jack Fish lived at 10 Sparling Street, Latchford, Warrington: Alfred Mather, head of house, aged 29, blacksmith, born Warrington; Elizabeth Mather, wife, aged 29, born Warrington; John Mather, son, aged 7, born Warrington; Harold Mather, son, aged 6, born Warrington;
Alsie Mather, daughter, aged 3, born Warrington; Alfred Mather, son, aged two weeks, born Warrington; John Fish, boarder, aged 23, gas range fitter, born Runcorn.

The rest of the family lived at 7 Renshaw Street, Lostock Gralam:
Richard Fish, head of house, aged 45, chemical labourer, born Runcorn; Mary A. Fish, wife, aged 42, born Runcorn; Samuel H. Fish, son, aged 12, born Runcorn; Edward Fish, son, aged 6, born Runcorn; Edith Fish, daughter, aged 4, born Northwich; Mary A. Fish, daughter, aged 2, born Northwich; Eliza J. Altmark, daughter, aged 19, born Runcorn; John Altmark, son-in-law, aged 21, chemical labourer, born Frodsham; Miriam Altmark, granddaughter aged 11 months, born Northwich.

For the 1911 Census, Jack Fish lived at 10 York Street, Warrington, a dwelling with four rooms, as follows: Jack Fish, head of house, aged 32, range fitter, born Runcorn, Cheshire; Fanny Fish, wife, aged 31, married 10 years, born Warrington, Lancashire; Alice Fish, daughter, aged 8, born Warrington, Lancashire; Joseph Carr, boarder, single, aged 24, labourer, testing department, Richmond Stove Company, born Warrington, Lancashire.

The Census also recorded that Mr and Mrs Fish had had four children, but that three of them had died.

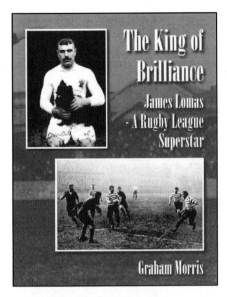

Great new book about one of the sport's genuine legends. James Lomas played for Bramley, Salford, Oldham and York, and won representative honours for Lancashire, Cumberland, England and Great Britain. He captained the first Lions team to tour Australia and New Zealand in 1910. This is the first biography of him.

Published in October 2011 at £16.95 (hardback). Copies available direct from London League Publications Ltd, PO Box 65784, London NW2 9NS (cheques payable to London League Publications Ltd); credit card orders via our website: www.llpshop.co.uk or from any bookshop

Rugby's Greatest Mystery
Who really was F.S. Jackson?

A true life rugby detective story

This is the story of a man whose life was made up of mystery, intrigue and deception, but was also a Rugby Union star before the First World War. He played for Leicester and Cornwall when they won the 1908 County Championship. He was selected for the Anglo-Welsh Rugby Union tour to New Zealand and Australia in 1908. However, the RFU recalled him from the tour and banned him from the sport over allegations that he was a professional player, and had played for Swinton in the Northern Union. The scandal around his suspension from rugby union caused great problems for the RFU and almost saw a further split in the game.

He then played Rugby League for New Zealand, against the British Lions in 1910. After the First World War he was reinstated by the New Zealand RU, became an East Coast selector and saw his son play for the All Blacks. For around 60 years he used the name Frederick Stanley Jackson, even though it was not his given name. When he died in 1957 he took to the grave his true identity. Even his family knew little about his early years in England, or even where he came from. **It was a mystery that remained unresolved until now.** The book also includes an analysis of the development of Leicester Tigers RFC up to the First World War.

Published in March 2012 at £12.95. Copies available direct from
London League Publications Ltd, PO Box 65784, London NW2 9NS
(cheques payable to London League Publications Ltd);
credit card orders via our website: www.llpshop.co.uk or from any bookshop.